FROM THE BOG TO BOSTON

A 20ᵀᴴ CENTURY IRISH JOURNEY

KATHLEEN T. CUMMINGS

ACKNOWLEDGEMENTS

Working with my father and mother on this book was a labor of love; traveling back through their lives has greatly enriched mine. I am deeply sorry that my parents did not live to see this work completed as they would have been thrilled and proud. This effort started as a vehicle to capture my parents' history for their grandchildren: Greg, Lauren, Matt, Steve, Bonnie, Danny, Mike, Elizabeth, Drew, and Larry. Along the way, however, it turned into much more, and I am grateful to so many people who helped with this undertaking.

Throughout his life my late Uncle Mike appreciated the value of documenting and sharing our family's history and he provided me with valuable material for chapters one and two. My Uncle Paddy, who lives in Ireland, also furnished me with key documents, photos, and his invaluable insights. My Aunts, the late Mary Finneran and Peggy Martyn also shared their memories and reflections. My sisters, Noreen and Lynda, have been supportive of me and this effort in ways words could never capture. My brother Larry, with his truly Irish sense of humor and earnest encouragement, was always enthusiastic about this project. My sister-in-law Ginny (Herman) Cummings and my brothers-in-law, Don Jordan and Peter Schablik, supported this effort with love and good humor.

In addition to family, I have been the beneficiary of a number of friendships that have both supported and shaped my life. In particular, I want to thank Maureen Sullivan and Pat Black for their unwavering support of this project.

When my youngest son, Drew, was in his sophomore year at Boston College High School, he came home excited to tell me about his English teacher, Mr. Frost. Drew described Mr. Frost as the "hardest teacher" he had ever had, and Drew clearly respected and admired him. Mr. Frost had a way of bringing out the best in my son, and Drew was privileged to have had classes with him in both his sophomore and senior years. Mr. Frost helped my son become a better writer, student, and person. Mr. Frost became Dr. Frost the year my son graduated from BC High, and he graciously agreed to edit this book. Michael Frost and I worked together toward the end of this project, and I am grateful to him for his careful editing eye and thoughtful critique. Thank you, Dr. Michael Frost for what you did for my son, and for me.

Finally, my children, Lauren and her husband Jimmy Lorentz, Matthew and his wife Dierdre (Connelly), Drew, and my grandchildren Beckham, Matthew and Mairéad grace every page of this book. My pride in them is boundless and my love for them has encouraged me to capture our shared Irish history.

Kathleen T. Cummings
Naples Florida
November 2023

Dedication

For my grandchildren who never got to hear the stories

Copyright © 2023 Kathleen T Cummings All rights reserved

No part of this publication may be reproduced, distributed, or transmitted in any form or by any means, including photocopying, recording, or other electronic or mechanical methods, without the prior permission of the author, except in the case of brief quotations embodied in reviews and certain other non-commercial uses permitted by copyright law.

ISBN: 979-8-9899273-1-9

TABLE OF CONTENTS

ACKNOWLEDGEMENTS	3
INTRODUCTION	9
TIMELINE	15
CHAPTER ONE: NO IRISH NEED APPLY	17
CHAPTER TWO: HIMSELF, HERSELF AND THE CHILDREN	31
CHAPTER THREE: FOUR LADS IN A BED	43
CHAPTER FOUR: SEX IS ONLY FOR ANIMALS	59
CHAPTER FIVE: JESUS, MARY AND JOSEPH AND MY SMALL WORLD	71
CHAPTER SIX: ONE SIZE DOESN'T FIT ALL	83
CHAPTER SEVEN: LET'S HAVE A BALL	95

CHAPTER EIGHT:
AND THEN THERE WERE TWO 105

CHAPTER NINE:
SAINT ANTHONY HELP ME–I WASN'T READY FOR THIS 115

CHAPTER TEN:
A NEW NAME IN THE LAND OF OPPORTUNITY 125

CHAPTER ELEVEN:
HOW THE IRISH BECAME WHITE 135

CHAPTER TWELVE:
ELIZABETH, THE KERRY GIRL 147

CHAPTER THIRTEEN:
"THE GIRL DOWN THE ROAD": ELIZABETH'S SHAMEFUL SECRET   161

CHAPTER FOURTEEN:
COOKIN', CLEANIN' AND LOOKIN' FOR A HUSBAND IN BOSTON 171

CHAPTER FIFTEEN:
BUILDING A FAMILY WITHOUT A SAFETY NET 181

CHAPTER SIXTEEN:
WORLDS APART: RAISING CHILDREN IN
THE ERA OF SEX, DRUGS AND ROCK'N ROLL 191

CHAPTER SEVENTEEN:
YOU'RE NOT IN IRELAND ANYMORE 203

CHAPTER EIGHTEEN:
REMOVING THE STRAITJACKET 213

EPILOGUE 223

INTRODUCTION

I grew up listening to my father tell stories about the *old country;* like many immigrants, the *old country* was the affectionate term he used for his homeland. Some of his stories were clearly tales, exaggerated truths designed to entertain in the Irish tradition of *chats around the hearth,* while others were his recollections of his journey into adulthood. It was a journey, which began in Bornacurra, Ireland in the 1930s, transitioned to Manchester, England and ended in Boston in the early 1950s. I listened many times to his stories, which were repeated over the years at family events, especially when a newcomer arrived. Some made you laugh so hard it hurt and some made you cry, but there were also those stories that left you shocked and speechless. Together, they tell of lives marked by physical labor, harsh Irish-Catholicism, strong family bonds, and an unwavering desire to overcome fear and insecurity in a new world.

My mother faced similar challenges, although unlike my father she was a reluctant storyteller. Her historical roots were given expression in private, and only after much coaxing from her children and grandchildren. Although there are expected parallels in their childhood experiences, especially the omnipresence of the

Catholic Church in Ireland, there are clear gendered distinctions. Like my father, my mother's experiences reveal the harsh realities that fashioned a cultural straitjacket of sorts, one she continued to wear in her new home in America. But unlike my father, my mother traveled to her new world harboring a deep secret. Her Irish upbringing, although kinder in many respects than my father's, set her adrift across the Atlantic with a deep sense of insecurity and shame.

Although this book is based on oral histories, a collection of my parent's stories, it is also grounded in historical scholarship that traces the intersection of histories of the Irish and, particularly, the Irish in America. My parents were born into a homogeneous, agricultural world where daily life was centered in small villages, transportation was on foot, bicycle or horse, and communication was verbal and face-to-face. They traveled across an ocean and attempted to find a comfort zone in Boston's Irish community. A cultural haven amid a rapidly expanding economy, Boston was home to many Irish immigrants in the 1950s. But try as they did, Boston's Irish could not insulate themselves from the forces that tore through the United States in the ensuing 1960s and beyond. How they removed---voluntarily or otherwise--their cultural straitjackets, defined the Irish experience in America. Although the following presents intimate portraits, my parents' story will undoubtedly resonate with other immigrant families. America is a land of immigrants who traded one world for another and often created family lives that would bear no resemblance to the worlds they left behind.

As my parents started their new family in America, they soon realized that their children did not experience being Irish in the ways that were familiar to them. My siblings and I were first and foremost Americans. We embraced American music, dance, sports, and popular culture. We pursued our individual interests, while attending the occasional extended family gathering. But extended family reunions became rare as we started families of our own. We pushed on with our American lives, and while we may have celebrated Saint Patrick's Day, we were largely Irish in name only. Yet, as I grew older, my desire to explore my parents' history was compelling enough for me to write this book.

I was driven by the personal desire to engage my family's history in a deep, textured, and honest way. I appreciate that we tend to be more interested in our history as we grow older. By the time my grandchildren will be old enough to ask questions about their great grandparents, I likely won't be here to answer them. In part, this work is my legacy to them, a place where they can come and visit their family history and where they can hear my voice. But this effort is also a product of my formal training in graduate school where I studied history at both Boston College and Brandeis University.

As an historian, I have always argued that we cannot fully appreciate the complexities of our present time if we do not attempt to understand our past. I use the word "attempt," because what we know for sure is dependent upon the myriad sources that we use to fashion an historical narrative. In this work, I rely on oral histories, primary sources, records that have given me direct access to my parents' lives and, secondary sources, historical scholarship that intersects with the themes of this work. In my father's case, the early sources are more abundant than what existed for my mother. As a consequence, the narrative's length favors my father's story. At the same time, however, both their early narratives are richly captured in ways that are both historically accurate and personally compelling.

The year my father died, I spent three weeks in Ireland, accompanied by my youngest son and nephew. The boys were the youngest of our parents' grandchildren, and my nephew carries my father's name. My mother was still alive, and she arranged a visit with her extended relatives in Kerry. We then traveled to my dad's home where we celebrated a dedicated mass in my father's honor at the small church where he had been baptized. On our way into church, we passed through the adjoining cemetery, and identified several headstones that carry the names of our ancestors. My Uncle Paddy, his children and grandchildren, the local parish priest, and my father's sole-surviving elementary school chum, Paddy Killea, joined us. After mass, I hosted a dinner celebration at a cottage I had rented where we listened to stories about my dad's youth. The next day, I walked through the bogs where my dad had worked as a young lad, and I put some of the bog into a sealed bag. When I returned home, my aunts and I sprinkled the bog remnants over my father's grave. I felt as though I had brought a piece of my father's home back to his American resting place; and in the process, I had reconnected my father with the bogs he loved so much.

History often ignores the story of the ordinary, choosing to recount the lives of those who "made a difference" or altered the course of events. Typical history courses are frequently organized around elections, wars and economic and social movements. While students often read in depth about "famous" individuals, ordinary lives are often relegated to statistics. We learn what percentage of people were unemployed, emigrated or voted for a specific party. But their lives rarely come to life in our history lessons, as if we have nothing to learn from the overwhelming majority of people who inhabited our shared world and shaped our historical narrative. Yet it is within the rich fabric of everyday life that we meet our collective past, come to terms with the present and find hope for our future. My parents' words are italicized within each subsequent chapter, and I have supplied the context for their words. I invite you to join my parents and me as we go back in time and travel from the top of the Irish bog to Boston.

TIMELINE

- 1892 Paddy Kilcommins, born in Galway, Ireland
- 1894 Katherine Carey born in Kerry, Ireland
- 1895 Nora Doyle born in Galway, Ireland
- 1896 Dan Carey born in Kerry, Ireland
- 1914 Paddy Kilcommins emigrates to Boston, changing his surname to Cummings
- 1914 World War I begins
- 1915 Nora Doyle emigrates to Boston
- 1915 Katherine Carey emigrates to Boston
- 1916 Easter Uprising in Ireland
- 1918 World War I ends
- 1922 Paddy Cummings returns to Ireland and resumes Kilcommins as his surname
- 1922 Irish Civil War begins
- 1922 Irish free state is established
- 1923 Nora Doyle returns to Ireland
- 1923 Paddy Kilcommins and Nora Doyle marry
- 1923 Irish Civil War ends
- 1924 Katherine Carey returns to Ireland
- 1924 Katherine Carey marries Dan Carey

- 1927 Eamon de Valera installed as president of Ireland
- 1929 Great Depression begins
- 1932 Lawrence Cummings is born
- 1932 Ireland's Economic War with Great Britain begins
- 1934 Elizabeth Carey is born in Kerry, Ireland
- 1938 Ireland's Economic War with Great Britain ends
- 1939 Great Depression ends
- 1939 World War II begins
- 1945 World War II ends
- 1953 Lawrence Cummings emigrates to Manchester, England
- 1953 Elizabeth Carey emigrates to Boston
- 1954 Lawrence Cummings emigrates to Boston
- 1955 Vietnam War begins
- 1957 Lawrence Cummings and Elizabeth Carey marry
- 1958 Noreen Cummings is born
- 1959 Kathleen Cummings is born
- 1962 Lynda Cummings is born
- 1964 Civil Rights Act passed
- 1969 Lawrence Cummings, Jr. is born
- 1975 Vietnam War ends

CHAPTER ONE:
NO IRISH NEED APPLY

Dad was no farmer; he should never have gone back home. (Larry Cummings)

It was not a foregone conclusion that my father should be born in Ireland and not the United States. Both his father and mother had lived in the United States for almost a decade when his father was summoned home in 1922. The eldest of seven brothers and one sister, the 30-year-old Paddy Cummings was expected to carry on the family name and take over *the place*. Although he hated farming and wanted to stay in America, Paddy was expected to do right by his family.

In the Irish countryside in the 1920s *to do right* was defined, not by the individual in concert with his family, but by traditions passed from one generation to another for as far back as anyone could remember. There was no question that it would have been a disgrace to the family name had Paddy refused to return home; that it wasn't his home anymore, nor a home he wanted, didn't matter. His father had been clear; if Paddy didn't return, *he'd put the place up on the tree.*

Paddy understood his father's threat to sell the family farm. In a time when land was the source of sustenance and the symbol of a family's worth in a village community, the idea that his father would even threaten to sell suggested the anger he must have felt toward a son who would even consider flouting tradition. That Paddy would even consider refusing his father suggests he had much to lose.

At the time Paddy got the final word from his father, he was firmly entrenched in his new American home. After processing at Ellis Island, New York, a 22-year-old Paddy arrived in Boston, Massachusetts in 1914. He promptly anglicized his surname, changing it from Kilcommins to Cummings as his uncles in America had done before him. Several years later, Paddy's brothers would similarly change their surname when they made their permanent homes in America. The practice was continued by my father's generation as he and his siblings took the Cummings name when they became American citizens.

As children, we were told my grandfather, his brothers, and the generation before them had changed the family name in order to find work. Signs stating, *No Irish Need Apply,* were everywhere, we were informed. In reality, there would have been no such signs in Boston when Paddy and his brothers arrived.[1] It is likely, however, the name change was initiated by the generation that came to America during the Great Hunger.

Between 1846 and 1854 a fungus devastated the potato crop in Ireland, which was the primary staple of the Irish diet. As a result,

---

[1] Such signs would have been prevalent in newspaper ads in the late 1830s and 1840s. See Thomas H. O'Connor, The *Boston Irish: A Political History*, Boston, 1995, Chapter 3 for a discussion of native Bostonian attitudes toward Irish immigrants. Richard Jensen, however, argues that signs stating, Irish need not apply, were never publicly displayed. See "No Irish Need Apply: The Myth of Victimization." *Journal of Social History*, December 2002.

one million people died from starvation and nearly two million sought to escape the devastation through emigration. Historians now label it the Great Hunger, as opposed to the Great Famine, because the term famine suggests there were no food crops available in Ireland. In fact, there were adequate food supplies for the population, but they were exported to Great Britain. [2]

Irish immigrants during the Great Hunger arrived in America, Great Britain and Australia in desperate conditions. Discrimination against the Irish was commonplace and *No Irish Need Apply,* was printed in some newspaper employment ads and put on signs in a number of store windows. Evidence suggests the practice was more widely visible in Great Britain than America, but nonetheless, the discrimination was universally real and impacted Irish arrivals. It is likely that the Kilcommins immigrants during that time period changed their name to Cummings in the hope of finding work. As later generations immigrated, they continued the practice of Anglicizing their surname. But Paddy Kilcommins did not change his name to find work. By the time he arrived during the second decade of the 20th century, Boston was a friendly community for Irish immigrants.

Just one year before Paddy arrived in Boston, the city had elected James Michael Curley, an Irish Catholic, to his first term as mayor. In the same year, Massachusetts elected its first Irish Catholic governor, David Ignatius Walsh. The Irish had, in fact,

---

[2] Historians continue to debate the extent to which the British government owns the devastation of the Great Hunger. On the 150th anniversary of the Great Hunger, the British government issued the following statement: "Those who governed in London at the time failed their people through standing by while a crop failure turned into a massive human tragedy". For a review of the historical discussion see: Daly, Mary E. "Historians and the Famine: A Beleaguered Species?" *Irish Historical Studies* 30, no. 120 (1997): 591-601.

dominated the political landscape of Boston since the late 1880s.[3] Irish American entry into high-profile politics was paralleled in Boston by a strong Irish presence in the upper ranks of the Catholic Church hierarchy.

William Henry O'Connell, elevated from Boston's Archbishop to Cardinal in 1911, had long pursued a *triumphalist, separatist Catholic subculture.*[4] Championing Catholic organizations for men, women and children, O'Connell had reinforced the parish as the center of Irish Catholic identity. When Paddy arrived in the city the Irish were a dominant presence. As one local journalist observed, *the once brow-beaten Irish Catholics have come into possession of Boston.*[5]

This is not to suggest that the Irish enjoyed economic dominance in Boston—they did not. A bifurcated society, Boston was politically dominated by the Irish and economically dominated by the *Yankees*. A uniquely accomplished and prestigious group, the Yankee aristocracy, or *Boston Brahmins,* as they were known, traced their ancestors to pre-revolutionary America. An educated, Protestant, and financially accomplished group, the Brahmins controlled Boston's economic landscape.[6] The dual reality fostered an inferiority complex among the Boston Irish, and it is likely that an Anglicized name gave Paddy Kilcommins and his brothers a sense of belonging in their new home, rather than more opportunity for work. He and other Irish arrivals in Boston during the first decades of the 20th century had many entry-level employment opportunities.

---

3   See William V. Shannon, *The American Irish*, New York, 1963.
4   O'Connor, p.197.
5   Ibid, p.198.
6   In addition to O'Connor, see Shannon, Chapter 11.

Paddy began his work life in America as a car cleaner for the Boston Elevated Railway Company (BERY), part of Boston's transit authority. The city was in the midst of tremendous physical expansion including the construction of new rapid transit tunnels, elevated railway lines, and surface routes. Paddy joined a number of Irishmen who worked for BERY, and he enjoyed the work, hoping to become a railcar driver. But a childhood accident, which resulted in a disability, prevented him from realizing his goal.

Sometime before his second birthday, Paddy stumbled into the open fireplace in the Kilcommins family's thatched cottage, permanently damaging two fingers on his right hand. Such accidents were likely common occurrences in homes throughout the Irish countryside. With an open fire burning most of the day to provide heat and a source for cooking, it is likely many children learned the dangers of fire the hard way. With neither hospitals, nor professional doctors nearby, his mother would have treated Paddy as best she could.

At the time Paddy was a young child rural Ireland was heavily influenced by folk medicine. That his mother prevented infection from spreading suggests she had acquired a commonsense approach to medical treatment. Her approach was undoubtedly a shared knowledge among other village women who, like Paddy's mother, routinely encountered such accidents.[7]

Paddy's disability prevented him from becoming a driver, but it did not discourage him. He soon left BERY, moving on to work at a local wool house. As the collection point for sheep's wool, it was mundane work at low pay. Paddy apparently regretted his

---

7   For a discussion of the historiography surrounding folk medicine in Ireland, see: Foley R. *Indigenous narratives of health: (re)placing folk-medicine within Irish health histories.* J Med Humanit. 2015 Mar;36(1):5-18.

decision to leave BERY and he returned at his first opportunity. Within months of accepting work at the wool house, Paddy was back at BERY working as a *starter,* directing trolley traffic. Although he'd never actually drive the trolleys, he'd earn more than he did as a car cleaner or wool house worker. He must have been satisfied with the work environment since he remained at BERY until he returned to Ireland in 1922.

To supplement his earnings Paddy worked evenings as a bartender at Greans Bar in the Roxbury section of Boston. Although the bar does not exist today, it was still there when my father came to America; and, like his father, he socialized there with his fellow Irishmen. For Paddy, bartending was as much about the social activity as it was a way to make extra cash.

Paddy was a solid, broad-shouldered young man who stood 5'9" tall with dark black hair and bright blue eyes. He had an outgoing personality and was known as a smart lad who loved to read and hated to farm. He lived with his aunt and uncle on his father's side of the family, and they became very attached to Paddy who they regarded as a hard worker and lively conversationalist. Paddy had a reputation as a good storyteller with a keen interest in politics. From across the bar, he likely engaged other Irishmen in the hot topics of the day—the Great War and Ireland's struggle for independence.

When Paddy was born in 1892, Ireland was part of the British Empire. Centuries of British exploitation, dating back to the 12th century, had left a legacy of hatred and mistrust. In the last years of the 19th century, however, England had softened its position vis-à-vis Ireland and allowed the resurgence of Irish culture in a movement known as *Irish Ireland.* Not surprisingly, in 1905 the movement was politicized with the formation of *Sinn Fein,* or *we ourselves.* Just as Paddy was coming into manhood, Ireland's quest for independence was launched.[8]

Before he emigrated to America, as a young adult Paddy would have been part of many *chats around the hearth,* as he joined his fellow villagers for discussions that spanned from cheerful anecdotes to serious political exchanges. In particular, Paddy would have heard oral histories that chronicled generations of Irish suffering at the hands of the British. Like his fellow villagers, Paddy would have been sympathetic toward the Irish movement for independence. But years of exploitation had also taught the Irish rural poor to make do with what they had and not challenge the status quo.

Since the 1600s the Kilcommins family had farmed in Bornacurra. Irish for *top of the bog,* Bornacurra was poor land that had been discarded by the English. But, since potatoes could be easily grown in the Irish climate, peasant farmers, like the Kilcommins, coveted the land as a source of sustenance and security. As long as taxes were paid, the family could farm relatively undisturbed. The Irish independence movement, although a source of pride, would also have been unsettling to village farmers.

Many villagers would have feared that a war for independence would leave them worse off. Colonialism dances alongside racism, and the British saw the Irish as an inferior race. Many Irish internalized this inferiority to a point where they were fearful of *stirring the pot.* As a consequence, for many, the goal was to just get along.

---

8   An excellent starting point for Ireland's political history is Gerry Desmond's, *Desmond's Concise History of Ireland,* 2000.

Paddy was preparing to leave for America when he heard the news that Europe had gone to war. England, realizing it had more important things to worry about than Irish independence, signed a treaty that granted Ireland the right to home rule at the end of what became known as the Great War. In response, 150,000 Irishmen enlisted in the English war effort. But Irish rebels, discontent with the treaty's timing and terms, took advantage of England's preoccupation with the war and planned to revolt. As Paddy left for his new home, the political climate in Ireland was heating up.

Ireland's revolution was launched just two years after Paddy made his home in Boston. Originally unpopular with the masses, the revolution garnered support after the Easter Uprising in 1916 where 112 British soldiers were killed. England responded by imposing Martial Law and secret executions of Irish rebels—without customary legal safeguards--transformed the rebels into martyrs and the Irish populace into rebel supporters. Although the world made peace in 1918, Ireland's political future remained unclear.

Eamon de Valera emerged as the de facto leader of the Irish rebel government seeking independence from Great Britain. De Valera had been born in New York, the son of an Irish mother and Spanish father. His uncle brought him back to Ireland when he was just two years old following the death of his father. Unable to provide for her son as a single parent in 1884, de Valera's mother sent him back to Limerick to be raised by her extended family. There, de Valera thrived, pursued university education and joined the cause of Irish independence. Sentenced to death for his involvement in the Easter Uprising, de Valera escaped execution and was imprisoned in England. Released in 1917 as part of a general amnesty for Irish political prisoners, de Valera embarked on a career in politics and became instantly popular with the masses.[9] In 1919, de Valera came to America on a fundraising trip, and gave his first major speech at Boston's Fenway Park.[10]

Fenway Park opened just seven years before de Valera spoke at the venue. Today, the park is the oldest major league baseball stadium still in use. In 1919, the park hosted an average of 6,000 fans for home games. Nine months before de Valera spoke, the park swelled to 15,000 fans who watched the Red Sox defeat the Chicago Cubs in the 1918 World Series with Babe Ruth on the roster.

But on June 29, 1919, some 40,000 supporters flooded the gates at Fenway Park to hear de Valera speak. Undoubtedly, Paddy Cummings was among them. He may have joined the men and women who stormed the field as the park's 27,000 seats quickly filled. There, he listened to de Valera tell America: *The man who established your republic sought the aid of France. I seek the aid of America.*[11]

De Valera's American fundraising efforts certainly benefited from President Woodrow Wilson's campaign to ensure self-determination for all states. As the peace terms of the Great War were being negotiated, Wilson had set forth his *Fourteen Points* where he argued: *National aspirations must be respected; people may now be dominated and governed only by their own*

---

[9] Schmuhl, Robert. "Eamon de Valera: Man of Mystery." *Irish America*, February/March 2016.

[10] See, Eamon de Valera's visit to Boston in 1919 and 100 years of Irish-US relations. July 9, 2019. https://www.dfa.ie/irish-embassy/usa/about-us/ambassador/ambassadors-blog/blog/eamon-de-valeras-visit-to-boston-in-1919-and-100-years-of-irish-us-relations.html.

[11] Krebs, Albin. "Eamon de Valera, 92, Dies; Lifelong Fighter for the Irish." *New York Times*, August 30, 1975. For an engaging and thorough account of De Valera's American fundraising trip, see Hannigan, Dave. *De Valera in America*. Palgrave MacMillan, 2010.

consent.[12] De Valera echoed Wilson's belief in the necessity of self-determination in his speeches and, in the process, he captured both the hearts and dollars of his American audiences.

But Ireland's independence movement split over the terms of the country's treaty with England. The year Paddy's father wrote for his return, Ireland entered a period of civil war with the Irish Parliament and Michael Collins on one side and Eamon de Valera and his supporters on the other. Collins' assassination left de Valera the undisputed leader of the newly emerging republic.

The Civil War ended in 1923, the year after Paddy returned home. De Valera would not take the oath of office until 1927, but the fighting was over and Ireland—save Ulster County—could finally celebrate home rule. Although Paddy was returning to a different political world than the one that he had left a decade earlier, Irish independence did not serve as an incentive for him to return home.

The poor in Ireland, as elsewhere, typically lived life in the short run. Life decisions were based on economic necessity, not politics. Like his fellow villagers, Paddy's initial decision to emigrate was an economic one. Although he would have been proud of Ireland's newfound freedom, it would not change the practical circumstances of village farm life.

Paddy—like most Irish in America—understood that political freedom in his homeland would not immediately translate into economic opportunity. The Irish countryside, especially in villages like Bornacurra, County Galway, miles from Dublin, was a poor place. Irish independence did not serve as an impetus for reverse immigration. The Irish in America saw their new home as the land

---

12   President Wilson's Address to Congress Analyzing German and Austrian Peace Utterances. February 1918 (Retrieved, 2023).

of opportunity and Paddy Cummings was no different. He loved life in America and embraced the new opportunities he found in Boston. That he became an American citizen in 1919 confirmed his desire to remain in the states. Unquestionably, returning to Ireland would have been very difficult for Paddy. It would have been made easier, however, once his girlfriend, Nora Doyle, had agreed to join him as his wife.

The Irish had a bit of trouble expressin' feelin's, especially back then. When my father proposed to my mother, he wrote her a letter invitin' Ma'am to be his wife and share his place and assured her in the letter that "she knew all the rest." (Larry Cummings)

Honora Doyle was a petite, pretty 27-year-old redhead who, like many Irish immigrant women, worked as a live-in servant in Boston. She was 20 years old when she arrived in America on the R.M.S. Lusitania in April 1915. As history played out, it would be the final voyage for the Lusitania as it was torpedoed off the coast of Cork in May 1915 by a German U-20 boat and sank within eighteen minutes. The United States declared war on Germany two years later.[13] By then, Honora, or Nora as she preferred, had settled into life in America.

Nora was one of ten siblings born to Patrick and Bridget Doyle in Newbridge, Ireland. On the younger end of the brood, Nora had several brothers and sisters in America when she arrived, and they welcomed her, helping her to find employment. She quickly went to work for the Prendergast family on Bay State Road in Boston.[14]

---

13 For an engaging narrative of the sinking of the Lusitania, see Erik Larson, *Dead Wake: The Last Crossing of the Lusitania*, Broadway Books, 2016.

14 There were a number of prominent Prendergast family members is Boston at the time. We know of Nora's work in one home because she communicated as much to her family. Irish women in America had made up the most significant number of domestics since the mid 1800s, see Oscar Handlin, *Boston's Immigrants, 1790-1865*. Cambridge, 1941.

Nora's schedule was typical; she worked six days a week, twelve hours per-day, with one evening and one day off each week. Her time off, however, was suspended in the summer since Nora served a family with a home on Cape Cod. Each summer Nora and the Prendergast family would journey by car to the Cape where she would remain until Labor Day. Nora hated the isolation of the Cape as she missed the Irish socials and the opportunity to meet eligible Irish men.

Nora looked forward to the day she would marry and start a family of her own. It was her sister who facilitated the first meeting between Nora and a young man she viewed as a potential husband, Paddy Cummings. There would be no question that her future husband would be Irish. Whether or not she would stay permanently in America, however, was not settled in Nora's mind. Although she had become an American citizen and enjoyed the social activity in the city, Nora missed Ireland. Unlike Paddy, Nora loved farming. When Paddy told her that he was going back home and would write for her, Nora indicated she would be inclined to accept his proposal.

Marrying a man *with a place* was an honor for an Irish girl and Nora would likely have been very excited about returning home. She would not go back empty-handed, however. Nora would be expected to bring a dowry; in her case, all the money she had saved since coming to America. A frugal woman, over the course of several years Nora had saved several hundred dollars—a fortune by the day's standards. She would surrender every penny to Paddy's parents when she returned to Ireland. Later, they would give the money to their only daughter so that she, too, could *buy her way into a place.*

Paddy wrote to Nora shortly after he arrived in Ireland. The Irish had difficulty showing affection, particularly between genders. The custom of referring to one's spouse in the third person, as *himself* or *herself* suggests the desire to keep even intimate relationships at an emotionally comfortable distance. Paddy's letter to Nora was simple, asking her to be his wife and share his place. Finally, he assured her *you know all the rest*. One can only assume *the rest* was code for the loving words he could not bring himself to write. It was a language Nora understood and she promptly planned her departure from Boston back to her homeland and a new life as a married woman. Before she departed, however, her friends held a celebration in her honor.

Nora's friends were all Irish immigrant women who also worked as servants in affluent Boston-area homes. They understood each other, supported their shared challenges as domestic workers, and had fun together with their limited time off. While we will never know for certain, it may have been that among the guests at Nora's farewell celebration was a fellow Irish immigrant, Katherine Carey.

Katherine and Nora both arrived in Boston the same year, 1915, and it is possible, even likely, that the two women met. It was customary for the Boston-area domestics to gather at the local hall and celebrate a life-changing event, like Nora's engagement and impending departure back to Ireland. What they could not have known, however, was that Nora and Katherine would have a future connection as the mothers of my parents, Larry and Betty.

But in the meantime, Katherine Carey went back to work unaware that circumstances in her life would similarly lead her back to Ireland in the distant future. And Nora hugged all of her friends and said good-bye, knowing she would never see them again. There would have been the typical promises of *I'll write you,* but those promises would fade in time. Some of her friends may even have questioned Nora about the soundness of her decision and encouraged her to stay in the States. In that moment, however, Nora was excited about her new life as a married woman back in the land she loved. My grandmother packed her belongings, holding tightly to her dowry, leaving America, her friends, and all its promises behind as she headed back to Ireland.

CHAPTER TWO:
HIMSELF, HERSELF AND THE CHILDREN

It wasn't easy on Ma'am, coming into another woman's home. When you think of it, my mother couldn't even name her own children. (Larry Cummings)

Home for Paddy and Nora was Bornacurra, a small village with a dozen homes, just three miles from where Nora was born in Newbridge. Once back in Ireland, Paddy reverted to Kilcommins as his surname and when he married Nora Doyle in November 1923 in a simple church ceremony, they became Mr. and Mrs. Patrick Kilcommins, settling into his parents' home.

The Kilcommins house was impressive by the day's rural standards; it possessed two-stories with four rooms and a slate roof. Two fireplaces provided heating and a place to cook. A nearby well provided water for drinking, cooking and the occasional bath. Since there was no indoor plumbing and no designated outhouse, bathroom activities were carried out along the edge of the farm.

The Kilcommins family was among the first in the village to move from a thatched cottage to a cement structure and slate roof, a trend that occurred throughout rural Ireland in the 1920s.[15] The original thatched cottage remained and was used as a barn. The new home, however, was not well constructed; in fact, neither fireplace functioned properly. The kitchen hearth—the center of family life--filled the Kilcommins first floor with smoke every time the fire was lit. This necessitated that doors and windows remained open during the day, despite weather conditions.

For Paddy and Nora, their new home meant a step down from their American dwellings where each had enjoyed a shared, indoor toilet. Never again in their lifetimes would they know such luxury. They likely also missed city life and all it had entailed like public transportation, movie houses, restaurants, bars, and dance halls.

But the newlyweds settled into their home with Paddy's parents and would shoulder the responsibility of carrying on the Kilcommins name and farming tradition in the Bornacurra village. Paddy's seven brothers—without places of their own to farm—had left for America. Nora's arrival and the surrender of her dowry provided Paddy's sister Margaret with a dowry of her own. She quickly departed Bornacurra and married a man with a place of his own in a nearby village.

For generations in rural Ireland a woman's parents provided a dowry for a daughter marrying a man destined to inherit his family farm. Nora's family, however, did not possess the resources to honor this tradition, and she was charged with securing her own dowry from the fortune she had saved in America. It seems Paddy's family was also incapable of furnishing their daughter with a dowry. While Paddy fell in love with Nora in Boston, his parents certainly approved their union in Ireland with the knowledge

---

15   Emma Byrne, *Irish Thatched Cottage: A Living Tradition.* The O'Brien Press, 2022.

that Nora would bring a dowry that they could transfer to their daughter Margaret, ensuring that she, too, could successfully marry a man with a farm. Women, like Nora and Margaret, who *married into a place* in the rural villages of Ireland surrendered dowries until the Catholic Church discouraged the practice in the 1940s.[16]

Nora always resented the fortune she had been forced to surrender to her sister-in-law; it was a transaction she talked about with great passion and disdain for years. Moving into her mother-in-law's home was not easy but giving up every penny she had earned and saved through hard work and sacrifice was excruciatingly painful.

Adding to Nora's frustration was the Irish tradition that allowed her mother-in-law to name her children. Over the course of sixteen years Nora gave birth to eight children, six sons and two daughters. Nora's mother-in-law gave each child a family name drawn from a small pool, used repeatedly by the Kilcommins family for generations. As a result, the birth of Nora's children, Michael, Matthew, Mary, Margaret, John, Lawrence, Thomas, and Patrick, brought both joy and resentment to Nora.

A woman wouldn't go into church showin'. It would have caused a lot of talk. After mass, all the men would be talkin' and pointin', "Did you see your one?" (Larry Cummings)

Nora became pregnant just weeks after her wedding day in 1923. Pregnancy did little to alter a woman's daily routine in the Irish countryside and Nora would have continued to participate in both farming and household chores. In fact, little would change until her third trimester, when Nora would stay close to home. It

---

16 Luddy, M., & O'Dowd, M. Marriage in Ireland, 1660-1925. In *Marriage in Ireland, 1660-1925* (pp. l-li). Cambridge: Cambridge University Press, 2020.

was not for reasons of security that Nora stayed at home; rather, Nora stayed in for *shame's sake.*

At that time, a pregnant woman would not attend Sunday mass once she was showing. If a woman dared to challenge the norm, the village men would point and chide, *did you see your one?* The colloquial translation of *your one* would have been something akin to *the shameless woman who dared to enter the house of God with an enlarged abdomen---evidence that she had had sex.*

The Catholic Church in Ireland, particularly in the countryside, had grave difficulty coming to terms with human sexuality. Perceived as a dirty thing—even within the confines of marriage--village churches even forbade married men and women from sitting together during mass. It took a bold woman to enter a church obviously pregnant and Nora was not that bold. Nora and Paddy would have walked the two miles to mass together and split off to opposite sides when they arrived. By late in her second trimester, Nora would have stayed home, content to say the rosary on her special beads.

After her delivery, like other women, Nora visited the local priest to be *churched,* a blessing given by the Church to mothers after recovery from childbirth. Although scholars continue to debate the significance of *churching,*[17] rural Irish clearly viewed the practice as a necessary cleansing before a new mother could re-enter the house of God. Once *churched,* a woman was considered clean and eligible, once again, to attend mass and receive communion. But during her pregnancy Nora was likely more concerned about her upcoming delivery than the state of

---

[17] The debate splits between those who regard churching as a form of misogyny and those who find a deeper, spiritual, and cultural context for the practice. See, for example, Natalie Knödel in *The Thanksgiving of Women after Childbirth, commonly called The Churching of Women* (1995).

her soul. Undoubtedly, with her rosary beads in hand, Nora would have prayed to the Blessed Virgin Mary for a safe delivery.

Jesus, it was sad; everyone knew some woman who didn't make it through childbirth. (Larry Cummings)

Like all Irish women in the countryside, Nora gave birth at home. Trained nurses from the local towns acted as village midwives and assisted Nora and other village women. The practice had begun in 1918 with the Midwife Act and was later enhanced in 1925 with a Local Government Act that increased the availability of trained midwives in rural communities.[18] But advancements were slow in small, rural villages and at the time Nora started her family childbirth was still a frightening experience for a woman, especially her first time. Everyone knew some woman who had died from complications during childbirth. In spite of the risks, Nora came through her first delivery—as she would seven subsequent deliveries--with relative ease.

It didn't matter whether 'twas a boy or a girl, all little ones wore a dress. We didn't have any diapers; shit and piss just fell where it did, and the hens picked up after the tot. (Larry Cummings)

Like his brothers and sisters before him, my father, Nora and Paddy's sixth child, born in 1932, spent the first months of his life in his parents' bed. Nora breastfed all of her children, a practice that also served as a form of birth control since exclusive breastfeeding may prevent a woman from menstruating. Given that Nora's children arrived approximately two years apart, it would seem that breastfeeding not only provided her babies with

---

[18] DeFilippis, Michaela. Midwifery in Ireland, 2018. In *Midwifery Around the World*. https://medium.com/midwifery-around-the-world.

sustenance, but it also provided her with a limited ability to space her children.

At six months of age, my father was transferred to a large wooden cradle at the side of his parents' bed, where he would remain for another year. Diapers were a luxury that the poor Irish had neither the money, nor the time to embrace. Children of both sexes were kept in simple dresses until they could learn to go in the *pan* or a private spot outside. Since flooring was simple, either dirt or cement, a child went to the bathroom wherever it fell, and as my dad told us, *the hens picked up after them.*

Ma'am never got over Matt's death. Years later when I went home on my honeymoon, I found her cryin' after him. (Larry Cummings)

The unsanitary conditions coupled with the cold, damp weather in Ireland inevitably led to many childhood illnesses. In 1934, Nora and Paddy's seven-year-old son, Matthew, died after a bout of pneumonia. It was a heartbreak Nora carried with her throughout her life. Larry, a baby at the time, had no recollection of his brother, Matt. But he vividly remembered the pain his mother felt. Years after Matt's death, when my father returned to Ireland with my mother on their honeymoon, he found his mother sobbing. When Larry asked why she would be crying at such a happy time, Nora told him that she was so sad that Matt had been taken from her before he had the chance to marry and have a family of his own.

Following tradition at the time, Matthew Kilcommins' body was washed by three village women and laid upon Nora and Paddy's bed, dressed in a white gown. All the villagers would have come to the Kilcommins' home to express their sorrow. After the wake, Matthew's body was buried in the village cemetery next to the parish church.

Nora went on to bear more children, including two sons. Just two generations earlier, keeping with the village practice of the time, Matthew's name would have been given to Nora's next born son. My great, great-grandparents, for example, named their first-born son Anthony and following his death in infancy, called their next-born son Anthony as well. By the turn of the century, however, each child was regarded as unique, and the practice was discontinued. Nora and her mother-in-law would never have considered re-using Matt's name; clearly, they viewed Matthew as a cherished soul, irreplaceable in their family. But despite her heartache, Nora had little time to grieve. Even the death of a child did not stop the demanding routine of village farm life.

Farmin' was very hard work back then. We didn't have the modern tractors and the like that you had here in the States. All the children were expected to work. But Ma'am did the biggest share when we were young. God love Ma'am; she worked as hard as any man. (Larry Cummings)

Nora's life was centered on child-rearing and hard, physical work. For the first years of her marriage, the work was shared among Nora, Paddy, and his parents. But Paddy hated farming and several years into their marriage he was able to get work on the Irish County Council as a *ganger*, or supervisor. Ireland had entered a period of modernization, building up its infrastructure with a massive road construction project. Paddy worked as a bookkeeper, handling the payroll and ordering materials. The extra money was much needed at home, although there was a downside for Nora. Paddy enjoyed conversation and a nightly *pint* of Guinness with the *college lads,* the engineers who designed the roads. He similarly enjoyed the company of the local men in town at the public house, or *pub*, as the Irish called them. That Paddy had a full intellectual and social life apart from his wife and the farm to which he brought her, may have increased Nora's sense of isolation, and most certainly increased her workload.

The Doyles, Nora's parents, were known as a frugal, hard-working family throughout the surrounding villages. They tended to stay away from *the drink,* preferring to save money wherever they could. That Nora returned home with such a sizeable dowry seemed consistent with the community's assessment of her bloodline. It was reinforced by her work ethic. With a husband who disliked farming and worked daily at the County Council, Nora was left to handle the farm along with her children and aging in-laws.

Nora managed a sixteen-acre farm that produced sustenance levels of oats, barley, rye, potato, cabbage, and turnip. She also tended to about a half dozen pigs and cows. A few chickens and a rooster rounded out the family's farm animals. Her day began before sunrise when Nora prepared the morning meal, which generally consisted of oatmeal, and occasionally, eggs. Following breakfast, the older children would collect the eggs and feed the pigs. Nora milked the cows herself, taking the cream off the top to churn into butter. Dinner, served at 2:00 p.m. each day, consisted of potatoes and vegetables. On special occasions, like Christmas, the family enjoyed chicken or ham. Oatmeal was served again in the evening.

Ma'am would mend, but she wasn't much for makin' clothes. Now my grandmother was a talented seamstress; she would make pants for all the kids out of flour bags. (Larry Cummings)

In addition to her daily chores Nora would wash and mend the family clothes each week. Using a large iron pot, Nora would boil soap and water, dipping each article of clothing in turn. As each piece cooled, she would wring it out by hand and transfer it to a wooden rack to hang until dry. Clothing was passed from one child to the next and as worn spots appeared, mending also became necessary.

Money was tight for Nora and Paddy and store-bought clothing was a luxury they could not afford. Nora would routinely patch and mend, but she could not make clothing. My father's grandmother, however, was very skilled at transforming any available cloth into useful items. In particular, my father recalled that his grandmother routinely made pants, shirts, and bed sheets from large flour bags. Although the material was coarse, it served its purpose and held up well.

With a large family and little money, it was the creative and hard work of women, like Nora and her mother-in-law, who kept the family going. From morning till night, every day was filled with chores and child rearing. Unfortunately for Nora, there was little time for rest and relaxation.

Dad wasn't one to care much if Ma'am had a social life. He'd go off to a weddin' or a wake and leave her at home. (Larry Cummings)

Social activity in the Irish countryside centered on life events, particularly weddings and wakes. Both events were times to gather, eat, drink and *chat it up*. Since Paddy's position as a ganger allowed him to develop friendships beyond his village, he would often be invited to their social events. My father remembers that he generally went alone.

Although Nora's family was close by in the neighboring town of Newbridge, she rarely saw them. Paddy didn't enjoy the company of his wife's family, preferring to keep to his friends and his *own people*. At that time, custom did not mandate that a husband accommodate his wife's social needs, and as a result, Nora was in many ways a woman alone. Without the company of her own family and a sympathetic partner, her life consisted of childrearing and hard, physical labor conducted under her mother-in-law's watchful eye.

When my grandmother was dyin' she told me to pray to Saint Anthony and that if I did, he would always look after me. (Larry Cummings)

Nora's mother-in-law, like many Irish women of her time, was deeply religious. The Irish did not have a personal relationship with Jesus Christ; intermediates in the form of saints or the Virgin Mary provided their religious communications path. For my father, it was Saint Anthony. On her deathbed, his grandmother had told my father that he need only pray to Saint Anthony and his wishes would be granted. He took her words to heart. Although his mother had strong resentment against his grandmother, Larry—like his other siblings—loved her very much. Like many grandchildren, he remembers his grandmother as loving and affectionate, a woman to whom he often ran to escape his mother's beatings. While this type of protection undoubtedly further exacerbated the tension between Nora and her mother-in-law, it endeared her to her grandchildren. Many times, throughout my father's life, he would—as his grandmother instructed—pray to Saint Anthony. Larry credited his patron saint with saving him from ill many times in his life.

I remember the day we buried my grandmother; my mother went down on her knees, "Thank you God," she said, "I am a happy woman today." (Larry Cummings)

Mary (Connolly) Kilcommins died sixteen years after Nora married Paddy and moved into the Kilcommins' family home. Although Paddy and the children were heartbroken, Nora could not contain her sense of relief at the death of her mother-in-law, even in front of her children. Finally, Nora was the woman of her own home. Although her father-in-law was still alive, he had recently moved in with his daughter, following the death of her husband. He would remain with his daughter until his death, helping her manage the farm that she had inherited and would pass to her eldest son. Unfortunately for Nora, the relief she felt may have been short-lived. By the time Nora could assert herself as the woman of the house, it was overcrowded with children.

With only two small bedrooms in the Kilcommins' house, shared space was the only space available to any family member. Privacy was a luxury that few Irish farming families could afford. My father was born in 1932 and was old enough to leave the cradle and enter the *big bed* sometime between his first and second birthdays. When he got there, he was not alone.

CHAPTER THREE:
FOUR LADS IN A BED

We ate a lot of cabbage back then. As you might guess with the four of us lads in one bed, there'd be a bit of gas. One night I guess I was bit smellier than usual. My older brother, Mike, hung my arse out the window and told me if I farted again, he'd drop me down. (Larry Cummings)

Our attitudes towards spatial relationships change with each passing generation. I grew up sharing a small room with a younger sister in a house in which six people shared a bathroom. Among my friends, sharing a room was commonplace and private bathrooms were unheard of, a luxury reserved for the wealthy. My children, however, have always enjoyed bedrooms of their own. As teenagers, they also enjoyed private bathrooms. During a course I taught in American social history at a state college, I queried a class of freshmen about their childhood sleeping arrangements. Although the majority of students were not from affluent families--in fact, more than half were the first generation in their families to attend college--not one of the 30 had shared a bedroom. What I regarded as tight living in my youth must have seemed spacious to my father. The space that he had inhabited as a child would have been unbearable to me and unimaginable to my children. During his youth, my father's four-room house provided shelter for four adults and eight children. Such tight quarters were not uncommon in the Irish countryside where large families and small homes were the norm.

When Larry graduated to the *big bed,* he joined his older brothers, Mike and John. Within two years, his younger brother, Tom, was also sharing the same full-sized bed. Two lads at one end of the bed and two at the other left no room to roll over or to stretch out. One can only imagine the frustration the oldest boy, Mike, felt when my dad—a late bed-wetter—joined his brothers in the big bed. If one boy had a sour stomach, flu or cold, it was quickly shared by all. If one awoke from a bad dream, it is likely he woke the others as well. But there were also benefits to the boys' sleeping arrangement.

Given that the Kilcommins' home lacked central heat, and the boys' bedroom did not have a fireplace, the shared body heat benefited the boys at night. Ireland's climate is frequently cold and damp, especially in the winter. My father recalls there were no extra blankets on hand, so having warm bodies next to them at night insulated the brothers from the unforgiving climate. The bedroom also possessed the poor, rural version of today's ensuite.

The boys used a chamber pot, placed under the bed, when they needed to go in the middle of the night. Each morning the boys would take turns emptying the pot and gathering fresh straw for the mattress if needed. Seniority, of course, had its advantages; the younger lads generally performed the less glamorous chores, like emptying the pots, while the older siblings would restuff the mattress.

The intimacy that comes with sleeping side-by-side each night shaped the boys' relationships. Each brother knew as much as humanly possible about his male siblings; what frightened them and gave them bad dreams in the middle of the night, what foods agreed or disagreed with them, what made them laugh and cry, and what drove them crazy. That kind of intimacy manifested itself in two ways; the boys were at once fiercely loyal and endlessly argumentative. Throughout their lives, each one stepped up to lend a hand whenever another was in need, but they also cut each other down with a similar passion. Although age softened their arguments; when they were young, disagreements often played out physically.

Anger is a difficult emotion to contain when there is no place inside a home to be alone. The boys rumbled over any number of issues, both large and small. Age had its advantages and more often than not, the older brothers physically dominated the younger ones. But regardless of how they felt, angry or otherwise, when the day was done, the boys were shoulder to shoulder at night.

Nighttime rumbles were often curbed, however, by the boys' grandparents who also shared their small room. With just two bedrooms in the Kilcommins' house, space was at a premium. The boys' bedroom housed two beds—one for them and one for their grandparents. Each bed had a designated chamber pot, and the younger brothers were also charged with emptying their grandparents' pot each day. The home's second bedroom similarly housed two beds. The girls, Mary and Peggy, shared one bed while their parents, Paddy and Nora, shared the other. Like their brothers, the girls were similarly charged with emptying chamber pots from their room each morning.

Multiple generations sleeping side-by-side in a single room was common in the Irish countryside. Sleeping arrangements were assigned based on space requirements. Modesty, as we think of it today, didn't exist in my father's childhood world. Nothing was sacred when it came to family. What we think of today as private bathroom activities were carried out in full view of all in a room. Each member of the family, especially those who shared a room, experienced other members in the most intimate ways.

Well, there was the story about the schoolmaster who asked the children to name a fruit. One lad said, "candle." The schoolmaster told him that a candle was not a fruit, but the lad insisted. "Sure," the lad said, "just last night my father told my mother to blow out the candle and they'd have a bit." (Larry Cummings)

Although likely apocryphal, the story speaks to the reality that intimate relations among men and women did not take place in intimate settings. This was not, of course, specific to Ireland in the 1930s. Privacy, as we know it, is a relatively new construct. Although adults may have waited for children to fall asleep, there can be no doubt that children would have seen and heard adult sexuality.

What may seem shocking to us by today's privacy standards was widespread in the Irish countryside during my father's youth. Children would not have thought twice about sleeping in a room with their parents or grandparents—no one could have imagined it any other way. Unlike today, where children have access to the world via television and the Internet, the Irish countryside of the 1920s and 1930s was an isolated place. All the families in my father's village would have experienced life similarly. While there were a few more well-to-do families in the town who enjoyed more spacious living conditions, the Kilcommins family and their village neighbors never questioned their lack of privacy. Like other aspects of their lives, it was just the way things were. But was there a psychological cost to being raised without physical privacy?

There appears to be no research on space, living conditions and the potential psychological implications of lack of privacy in rural Ireland during my father's youth. This is not surprising since why would anyone study something that was *just the way things are*. But there is current research that has explored overcrowding, lack of privacy and multi-generational sleeping arrangements.

For example, in his study conducted in South Africa, researcher Gwandure examined third world living conditions which included lack of privacy and multi-generational sleeping arrangements.[19] He found an increase in anxiety, depression, and conduct disorders among children. In addition, he also referenced an earlier study that found an increase in incest among families that resorted to multi-generations sleeping in one room as they did in my father's time.[20] Los Angeles social science researchers, Mare and Solari, reported similar findings to Gwandure, but emphasized lack of academic performance and stressed the negative life-long implications associated with an early lack of privacy.[21]

It is challenging, perhaps impossible, to extrapolate recent research as a lens for examining life in rural Ireland during my father's youth. But it is also likely that the physicality of the boys' relationships was increased by their sleeping arrangement and lack of personal space. Their parents, however, would have

---

19 Gwandure, Calvin. "Life with Limited Privacy due to Housing Challenges: Impact on Children's Psychological Functioning." *African Safety Promotion: A Journal of Injury and Violence Prevention.* Vol. 7 No. 1 (2009).
20 Gwandure cited work done by Canadian clinical and forensic psychologist Dr. James R. Worling in 1995.
21 Mare, Robert D. and Solari, Claudia D. Housing Crowding effects on Children's Wellbeing. *Soc Sci Res.* 2012 March; 41(2): 464–476.

viewed it as *boys being boys,* and not given it a second thought. At the same time, I suspect the loyalty and devotion the brothers showed each other over the course of their lives was, in part, a result of their physical closeness. In any event, Paddy and Nora had more to worry about than sleeping arrangements, since the activities of daily life also proved challenging.

Well now, we never had a bath the way you think of a bath here in America. There was no tub or running water. Every week or so, you'd go out to the barn and Ma'am would heat some water over the fire, and you'd soap up and pour the water over you. (Larry Cummings)

Anyone who has raised sons will tell you that deodorant soaps are a must, especially during adolescence. One can only imagine the body odor that pervaded the small room inhabited by the boys and their grandparents. Bathing was a once-a-week ritual with little attention to detail. Parents and children alike simply stood in the barn and soaped their bodies with a basic, store-bought soap. A warm bucket of water was dumped over each in turn. Missing a weekly bath was not uncommon, especially in the winter months when frigid temperatures made bathing in the barn an uncomfortable experience. Given that the boys worked around pigs, chickens and cows, and hygiene was lacking, both odors and illnesses pervaded the Kilcommins' household.

I saw a doctor just once growin' up. I was very sick with ringworm and Ma'am took me to town to see the doctor. He treated my ringworm and told Ma'am that I had low blood and gave me castor oil. Ma'am told him that I ate more than ten lads. But the doctor told her it wasn't how much I ate, rather the quality of the food. We lived on potatoes back then. (Larry Cummings)

Among the many childhood diseases that were common in the Irish countryside my father experienced head lice, intestinal worms, ringworm and a host of flus and bacterial stomach illnesses. It was ringworm, however, a skin disease marked by round scaly patches that brought him to his first and only doctor's visit during his childhood. My father received an ointment to treat the fungus that caused his skin disease. But the doctor also observed that my father was anemic. His mother was shocked that her son who *ate as much as ten lads* could have *low blood*. Not unlike other village women, my grandmother focused on giving her children enough to eat. Even if Nora had possessed a fuller understanding of nutrition, she wouldn't have had the money to do anything about it. My father's family ate what was cheap and available; like generations before them, that consisted largely of potatoes.

Frequent intestinal disorders further exacerbated living conditions, and anemia resulted from the family's inadequate diet. Except during the especially cold months of winter, the children walked about barefoot. With human and animal waste underfoot, it was not surprising that parasites, in the form of worms, invaded the children's bodies. My father and his siblings, like the other village children, would frequently see worms in their feces. Since worms come out of the body in the warm environment of a bed, the closeness of the boys at night meant that once one boy was a host to worms, the others might quickly be invaded as well. As a result of these conditions the children were continually at risk for any number of illnesses. Given the lack of nutrition and medical care it is amazing that the Kilcommins family lost only one child.[22]

---

22 Information about the diseases referenced is available online at MEDLINE Plus, a service of the U.S. National Library of Medicine and the National Institutes of Health: http://medlineplus.gov/.

The dentist would come around to the school once a year. You got in line, and he'd pull any tooth that was bad. Only the girls got Novocain—there wasn't much of it and the thinkin' was that the boys could take the pain. Jesus, 'twas awful—I can remember lyin' and tellin' him all my teeth were fine. But he'd take a look and yank the rotten ones anyway. (Larry Cummings)

Dental hygiene was nonexistent in rural Ireland when my father was growing up. None of the Kilcommins family possessed a toothbrush or had even heard of toothpaste. In 1919 there were only 200 qualified dentists in the whole of Ireland and fully half were located in and around Dublin. Another 40 dentists were located in Northern Ireland, leaving little more than 40 to cover the rest of the country. While it started to improve gradually, it was little better by the time Nora and Paddy were raising their family.[23] It wasn't until 1960 that the Irish Health Act included fluoridation of water, a decade after it had been initiated in the United States, making a significant difference in the oral health of children.[24] My dad and his siblings were given a mixture of baking soda and water to wash out their mouths on bath day, and while this likely helped somewhat, it did not prevent rampant tooth decay. Some of Larry's most painful memories involved aching teeth. Larry vividly recalls a night he ran from the house and plunged his head into a cold barrel of water to find relief from a toothache.

In an effort to provide some measure of dental care, the national government sent a dentist once each year to local villages. The dentist's job was not to provide proactive education and

---

23   Cullen, Tom, Editor. History of the Irish Dental Association, 1922-1972 in *Journal of the Irish Dental Association*, 2013.
24   O'Mullane DM, Whelton HP, Costelloe P, Clarke D, McDermott S. Water fluoridation in Ireland. Community Dent Health. 1996 Sep;13 Suppl 2:38-41. PMID: 8897749.

cleaning materials, but to pull rotten teeth. Since Novocain was in short supply, boys were encouraged to *tough it out,* while girls would be given a small dose prior to the extraction. One can only imagine the horror that the little boys felt as they stood in line waiting to have a tooth pulled without the benefit of medication. For my father, he would swear his teeth were fine. But year after year, the dentist extracted one rotten tooth after another. By the time he left Ireland in his early twenties, Larry had lost eight teeth in all. But for many Irish children, toothaches were just one of many discomforts they had to endure.

Winters were cold and damp, and I didn't have a coat to wear. One Sunday Ma'am gave me her coat goin' to church. But I was awful embarrassed to wear a woman's coat in front of the other lads. On my way to church, just as soon as I was out of Ma'am's site, I threw the coat in the ditch. Ma'am nearly killed me when I got home. (Larry Cummings)

Ireland's damp, cool climate also exacerbated illness, particularly in the winter months. My father's brother, Matt, who died during childhood of pneumonia was infected during the middle of winter. Without the benefit of central heat and proper clothing, children were particularly cold from late fall until spring. Store-bought clothing was a luxury that the Kilcommins family could not afford. Nora did her best to see that each child had a coat—even going as far as to surrender her own. But teasing among children was common, and my father chose to freeze rather than be seen in his mother's coat.

I got my first suit when my cousin, Anthony, died from meningitis. It was a fine store-bought pants and jacket, and it came just in time to wear to my first communion. 'Twas the only store-bought clothin' I had growin' up; I felt so lucky. (Larry Cummings)

Paddy's only sister, Margaret, also lost a child in the cold, damp winter months. Anthony had been my father's age and they were about the same size; therefore, my father was the logical recipient of Anthony's clothing. That Anthony had a store-bought suit suggests Paddy's sister and her husband may have been better off than the Kilcommins family. My father rarely saw his cousin, at most a couple times each year; and although he received his first suit as a result of a tragedy, my father was overjoyed. Store-bought clothing was a symbol of affluence in the countryside and my father felt very proud wearing his new suit, especially on his first communion day. It would be the only time during his childhood that my father would experience the pride of wearing store-bought-clothing. Not until his arrival in England would my father actually own store-bought-clothing again.

Scarcity was a way of life for all rural villagers. While my father was born during the Great Depression, there wasn't a sense that things had gotten worse. The western economic changes certainly impacted Ireland, but it was not perceptible on a day-to-day level to rural, sustenance farmers. Life had largely been the same before and after the Depression.

In Ireland the Great Depression was characterized as an economic war with Great Britain, beginning the year my dad was born in 1932 and ending in 1938. The war had its roots in the disputed Anglo-Irish Settlement of 1921, which had provided for Irish land annuity payments to Great Britain. De Valera refused the payments, pursuing a protectionist economic agenda, and

Great Britain responded with penalty tariffs on Irish imports.[25] The economic war greatly impacted cattle exporters, but the rural poor in villages, like Bornacurra, were sustenance farmers who rarely ate meat much less exported it. While the trickling effects of the economic war seeped into small villages in rural Ireland, in reality, life during the Great Depression was little different than it had been in the 1920s. But while the 1930s didn't bring about economic changes for the Kilcommins family, it was a time of familial adjustments.

Grandad moved away to live with my Aunt Margaret after her husband died. I was young at the time, about eight or nine. She needed help around the farm and with all her brothers except Dad in America, Grandad was the only one who could help. After Grandad left my brother John moved into the bed with Grandma'am, giving Mike, Tom and me a bit more room. But Grandma'am had asthma and Ma'am always said that was why John was so much shorter than the rest of us boys. She claimed that Grandma'am took up all the oxygen and John didn't have enough to grow properly. (Larry Cummings)

It was not unusual for the Irish in the countryside to interpret certain phenomena within a context that we today would regard as nonscientific. How could one son be 5'4" tall while another was 6'1"? My grandmother looked for circumstances that were specific to my Uncle John.

As the recipient of Nora's dowry, Margaret Kilcommins, Paddy's only sister, married Patrick Hardiman and moved to a neighboring village. She and her husband had one child, and shortly thereafter, Patrick Hardiman died from a ruptured

---

25 Neary, J. Peter; Ó Gráda, Cormac, Protection, Economic War and Structural Change: The 1930s in Ireland. *Irish Historical Studies,* 27 (107): 250-266, 1991.

appendix. She quickly remarried Martin Heavey, who also owned a farm. Together, they had four more children. While the cause of death is uncertain, Martin Heavey died when the children were quite young, leaving Margaret in charge of both the farm she inherited from her first husband, and the farm she inherited from her second. With two farms to manage and five children to raise, Margaret needed help. It was her father who came to her assistance. He permanently left the Kilcommins family home in order to move-in with his daughter. He would ultimately die in her home at 91 years of age. The grandfather's departure meant that one of the boys could sleep in their grandmother's bed, giving the other three boys more room. Nora decided that John would sleep with his grandmother. Later, she would determine that John was so much shorter than her other sons because he had lost oxygen to his grandmother who suffered from asthma. For Nora, it seemed the only possible explanation for the fact that there was such a disparity in her sons' height.

The boys ranged in size from less than to greater than average, with my father falling in the middle measuring 5'9". All the boys were slim; in fact, the sole photograph that exists reveals that my father was quite thin. The girls were average height and also slender. They all had blue eyes and hair color ranged from my Mike's blonde color to my father's deep black. Over the course of their lives my father and his siblings have debated just who is a Doyle and who is a Kilcommins. The Doyles tended to be red headed, while the Kilcommins clan had dark hair, though both families had blue eyes. But observers noted that all of the siblings looked very much alike. In a room full of people, you could easily tell that they were related. Their differences were related more to their personalities and the roles each played in the family. Their roles were forged in childhood and, not surprisingly, carried over into adulthood.

Dad was off most of the day and the discipline was done by my older brother Mike. He was the smart one in the family and had no tolerance for my mischief. (Larry Cummings)

The phrase *it takes a village* would have resonated with the Kilcommins family and their village neighbors. Discipline—defined during my father's childhood as corporal punishment--was doled out by parents, adult neighbors, the local parish priest, the schoolmaster, and older siblings. No one questioned an adult's ability to discipline any child in the village. At home, it was my father's oldest brother, Mike, who *checked* the younger boys.

Mike enjoyed all the characteristics that personify authority; he was tall, handsome, intelligent, and mature. He also wholeheartedly embraced the tenets of the Catholic Church. My father was younger, shorter, more a farmer than a student, and mischievous. But my father respected and feared his older brother. His bedmate at night, Mike was his parental figure during the day.

I got it in my mind that I would go after Mike. I waited in the barn and told John to be on the lookout. As soon as Mike entered the barn I jumped down from the loft and tackled him. John took off and I was no match for Mike alone. He quickly wrestled me to the ground and grabbed a pile of cow shit and shoved it in my mouth. I never went after him again. (Larry Cummings)

Larry's futile attempt to put Mike on notice that he was not a kid anymore failed miserably. Until he left for America at 24, Mike was more an authoritarian than a sibling where my father was concerned, a relationship that continued in America. Near his death, my Uncle Mike told my father he was sorry for the way he had treated my dad in his youth. My father loved his older brother and was always there for him in his long decline from Lou Gehrig's disease. He assured my uncle he had done nothing for which he needed to apologize, *Jesus Mike, 'twas the way things were,* he reassured him. Mike held his hand and nodded and together they shared a loving bond that brought peace and comfort to both brothers during my uncle's final days. But my father's eldest brother was hardly alone in his role as disciplinarian; rather, Mike was one of a number of authority figures who would check my father's propensity to get into trouble.

We had a town police officer that came out to the village on a motorcycle. It was the first time I had ever seen anythin' like it before. When the officer got off it and walked away, I couldn't resist jumpin' up on it. I managed to start the damn thing and I ended up in the ditch with the motorcycle on top of me. (Larry Cummings)

Larry had plenty of company when he got into a mischievous mood. Like the Kilcommins, neighboring village families had multiple children. There was no shortage of playmates during my father's youth. My father and his childhood friends engaged in antics that today we might regard as innocent fun. Life was simple; and serious temptations, like drugs and alcohol, didn't exist.

There were local pubs, of course, and some of the village men, like my grandfather, routinely visited for a pint. But there was no alcohol in the Kilcommins' home when my dad was growing up. As the children moved into their teens, they would meet after supper in large groups *up the road* to socialize. But alcohol would never be a part of their gatherings. In fact, my father had his first drink in America at the age of 24. Similarly, drugs were unheard of in my father's village. Some of the lads would occasionally have the opportunity to buy cigarettes, or *fags,* as they called them.

But money was tight and few in the younger generation became addicted as a result of the infrequent exposure.

Similarly, children in my dad's village were raised in an environment without many of the fears that today's children must absorb. There were no locks on the doors in the village since break-ins were unheard of. Childhood abductions, terrorism, school shootings and the like were unknown in my dad's youth. There was a veil of innocence in those times that offered a strong measure of security, albeit in the midst of scarcity.

Finally, no one in the village owned an automobile. In fact, prams or horse-drawn carriages, were a sign of affluence during my father's youth. As a result, children got around either on foot or on a bicycle. Bicycle parts were valuable items and were recycled and passed on from one sibling to another. A single home might have as many as two or three bicycles. Without high-speed transportation and in the absence of alcohol and drugs, parents in Bornacurra did not share the same types of concerns that today's parents face.

The one fear that parents consistently housed, however, was that their daughters might become pregnant. Pre-marital sex was taboo in the Irish countryside and stayed taboo well after my father had emigrated to America. An out-of-wedlock pregnancy devastated a girl's life and brought shame on her family. A boy who *got a girl in trouble* was similarly shunned within the village and prevented the boy from finding a suitable wife. As a consequence, the community went to extraordinary lengths to ensure that both girls and boys remained virgins until they married. As Larry transitioned from childhood to adolescence, he and his fellow village friends were inundated with warnings about the dangers of human sexuality.

CHAPTER FOUR:
SEX IS ONLY FOR ANIMALS

Sex was everywhere when Larry Cummings was growing up. Parents and grandparents shared bedrooms with children; animals were bred in barns and in fields; women gave birth to children at home. Yet human sexuality was a forbidden topic of discussion among Irish villagers. Parents did not discuss sex with their children in a direct manner; rather, messages about sexual relations were communicated through religious teachings and discipline. The Catholic Church's position resonated throughout village life--sex was exclusively for reproduction within the bounds of matrimony. Sexual transgressions would put young people on a road to eternal damnation and Irish priests and parents were ever vigilant in their effort to save young people from the fires of hell.

My dad was awfully worried about Mary and Peggy. One night he found out they had been down the road. When they got home, he beat the hell out of 'hem. (Larry Cummings)

Although both adolescent boys and girls were held responsible for abstinence, girls had the most to lose from an illegitimate pregnancy. As boys and girls became young men and women, they naturally sought out each other's company. Going *down the road* was code for meeting up with a date in private. Since private meetings might lead to kissing and perhaps more, parents were particularly cautious about their daughters' nighttime activities.

My father recalls the night his dad returned from town and overheard young couples laughing and kissing behind a ditch. When he got home and learned his daughters, Mary and Peggy, were not at home, he queried his wife about their whereabouts. Nora believed their daughters were visiting at a neighbor's house, but Paddy called her a fool and insisted that they were *down the road*. He waited up for the girls to return and, upon their arrival, both Mary and Peggy were punished physically. Paddy didn't give his daughters the benefit of the doubt; he didn't bother to ask where they had been. Fearful that they would cross a dangerous line, Paddy invoked corporal punishment, an accepted and widely practiced discipline in the Irish countryside during my father's youth. As in other village homes, the message in the Kilcommins' household was clear: If you engage in sexual activities with boys—even if you are suspected of doing so—you will pay dearly.

There can be no doubt that Paddy would have believed he acted in his daughters' best interest. Girls who went astray or, *dillies* as the villagers called them, were publicly shunned. No respectable family would allow their son to contemplate marriage to a young woman whose reputation was questionable. If a girl became pregnant and her pregnancy was not legitimated by marriage, she was often shipped off to a local convent, which also functioned as a home for unwed mothers.

Magdalene asylums, Catholic homes for unwed mothers, prostitutes and young women of *questionable reputation* existed in Ireland from the early 19th century through 1996 when the last asylum closed. There was an irony in the relationship between the Catholic nuns and their young charges. As chaste women married to Christ, nuns were the purest of the pure, a model of ideal feminine behavior. Having a daughter who became a nun was a symbol of a family's devotion to the faith and earned the family bragging rights. Conversely, unwed mothers and other young girls who crossed—or were thought to cross—the Church's strict line regarding pre-marital sexual relations, represented the dirtiest of women and brought shame upon their families.

Magdalene asylums, named for Mary Magdalene, the New Testament figure popularly but erroneously assumed to have been a prostitute, were notoriously cruel institutions.[26] Director Peter Mullan's controversial, critically acclaimed film, *The Magdalene Sisters* chronicles abuses of prostitutes, unwed mothers, and young women labeled sexually promiscuous in Ireland in the 1960s. Although a work of fiction, the film is based on survivor accounts. In response to the film, the American wing of the Sisters of Mercy issued a statement acknowledging that the Magdalene institutions represent a *time in the history of the Catholic Church and religious orders of which we are not proud.*[27]

Penitents, as the young women were called, were made to scrub floors, do commercial laundry, and perform countless other demanding chores. Pregnancy did not excuse a penitent from her work; she continued to carry her share of the load right up until she delivered. Isolated from the outside world, penitents were forbidden visitors and denied written correspondence through

---

26 See Frances Finnegan's, *Do Penance or Perish: A Study of Magdalene Asylums in Ireland* (2001) and Mary Raftery and Eoin O'Sullivan's, *Suffer the Little Children: The Inside Story of Ireland's Industrial Schools*, (2001).

27 The film debuted in 2002. See Greydanus, Steven D. *The Magdalene Sisters Controversy*, 2003.

the mail. They would be reminded over-and-over that they had broken the laws of God and must pray for forgiveness. As their time came near, professional physicians were called. Unlike local midwives who intimately understood how to assist deliveries, professional doctors sent women to bed and heavily medicated them, preferring to deliver with forceps. Unwed mothers, however, were denied medication as they had to physically feel the pain of their sins.

Stories about the horrific experiences of unwed mothers and girls of questionable reputation were whispered throughout the countryside. Real, imagined or exaggerated, these stories served an important function; they reinforced the need for chaste behavior and reminded young village teens that sexual transgressions might lead to a life of pain, humiliation and eternal damnation. Unwed mothers often spent years as penitents, long after their babies had been put up for adoption. Survivor accounts include reports of physical, psychological and sexual abuse.[28] If a woman did acquire a release, she frequently left for England or for the States. The local village regarded a *fallen woman* as a cancer that might spread if allowed to remain.[29]

With this in mind, Paddy would have made a severe impression on his daughters to prevent them from far worse treatment. Ensuring chaste behavior among daughters was first and foremost a good father's job in the Irish countryside. And when Paddy feared his girls were *up the road,* he delivered a powerful

---

[28] Fischer, Clara. "Gender, Nation, and the Politics of Shame: Magdalen Laundries and the Institutionalization of Feminine Transgression in Modern Ireland." *Signs* 41, no. 4 (2016): 821-43.

[29] In 2013 the Irish government conducted an official inquiry into the Magdalen Asylums and published its findings in the *McAlesse Report.* Following the report's publication, the government issued an official apology to the victims.

message. Paddy's message was echoed by all local institutions, especially the Catholic Church.

Ah, Jesus, we thought we'd burn in hell if we went off with a girl. It was the worst kind of sin. (Larry Cummings)

My father and the other village children believed that premarital sexual activity was a mortal sin—punished by an eternity in hell. Although there was a litany of transgressions that qualified as mortal sins, adolescent boys and girls understood that sexual transgressions were somehow *the worst of the worst*. Stern messages were delivered not only by parents but the parish priest who used carefully veiled words to warn young people about inappropriate sexual behavior.

"The priest would never say anythin' outright, of course, but he warned us about the sinful behavior of blaygards and dillies. It was hard right enough; you were scared to death but curious at the same time." (Larry Cummings)

At Sunday mass boys gathered on one side of the church and girls on the other, a practice which reinforced the sinful nature of intimate behavior. In Ireland, both promiscuous girls and boys had names, and dillies and blaygards were both going straight to hell. For young people who were connected---real or imagined—with sexual transgressions, the consequences were severe.

I recall the priest's cousin, Paddy Kilary, got a girl in trouble. She blamed it on Paddy Liroy—perhaps because he was first in line to a farm of land—or maybe because she was afraid of shamin' the priest. But Paddy Liroy swore to his father that it wasn't him and he stood by him. Later it came out that it was the priest's cousin who fathered the child. But no girl would dance with Paddy Liroy after that; he had to go far off to find a wife. (Larry Cummings)

Boys-will-be-boys might have been an accepted standard when it came to rough and tumble, but it was not the case when it came to sex. Adolescent boys, as well as girls, continually received messages about the virtues of chastity. Even when a boy was cleared of wrongdoing, he was still tainted by the initial charge. Charges of sexual misconduct were played out on a public stage where all villagers participated or at least observed. The drama served as a reminder to adolescents just what would happen if they went astray. The focus on sexual misconduct and the association with sex as a *dirty* practice often produced unsettling feelings among the young.

When Ma'am was pregnant with Paddy, Mike's friends teased him somethin' awful. "Your father got into your mother," they told him. After Paddy was born Mike refused to go up to Ma'am's room and see his new baby brother. Paddy was nearly six weeks before Mike would even look at him. (Larry Cummings)

My father's oldest brother, Mike, was fifteen when his mother became pregnant with her youngest child, Paddy. Like most children, Mike had grown up in a household that had not afforded adults sexual privacy. Nonetheless, the messages prohibiting sex were delivered in terms that caused young people to think of intercourse as *dirty*. The result was an inner tension or anxiety about what existed in the normal course of life and the ways in which society and the church categorized the behavior in pejorative terms. Mike hated being taunted by the other village boys, and he demonstrated his feelings by denying Paddy's existence. In time Mike acquiesced to the reality, but he was relieved that Paddy was Nora's last child.

Church teachings and parental discipline addressing sexual behavior were also echoed by the state. In her work on sexuality and the newly formed independent, Irish state, historian Maria Luddy found the two to be perfectly aligned:

Both the state and the church emphatically presented women's place as being in the home and the ideal role of the Irish woman was as mother. The idealization of motherhood was a significant feature of the rhetoric of politicians in the new Irish state; the female body and the maternal body, particularly in its unmarried condition, became a central focus of concern to the state and the church.[30]

The state routinely published sermons on sexuality in the form of pamphlets. And while women were critiqued for immodesty in fashion and for desiring to work outside the home, the primary focus was on their sexuality. Not only was premarital sex sinful, but it also threatened the very foundation of a free Ireland. As Dr. Thomas Patrick Gilmartin, Archbishop of Tuam noted in 1926, *the future of the country is bound up with the dignity and purity of the women of Ireland.*[31]

Historian Clara Fisher has argued that as Ireland became an independent country it sought to define itself against its former British identity. The colonizing British were impure and licentious, while the Irish were pure and virtuous. Chastity, particularly female chastity, became a central component of this newly emerging identity and was reinforced by Catholic social teachings. [32]

It is also likely that as a poor country, having the moral high ground gave the Irish a sense of national pride. While they may

---

30 Luddy, Maria. "Sex and the Single Girl in 1920s and 1930s Ireland." *The Irish Review (1986)*, no. 35 (2007): 79-91.
31 Ibid. p. 80.
32 Fischer, Clara. "Gender, Nation, and the Politics of Shame: Magdalen Laundries and the Institutionalization of Feminine Transgression in Modern Ireland." *Signs* 41, no. 4 (2016): 821-43.

not have been a rich country, they regarded themselves as morally superior, and morality was first and foremost about sexual purity. As a result, both politically and religiously, the message was clear and pervasive in Ireland, premarital sex was an egregious sin. But institutionalized fear about premarital sex didn't prevent adolescent curiosity.

We were touchin' and kissin' each other. We were a bunch of boys tryin' to figure out how you did it with the girls. Jesus, I have never told anyone this before. (Larry Cummings)

My father and I had many deeply personal conversations when I contemplated writing this book. I believed he had an easier time talking with me about uncomfortable subjects because I approached our talks from an academic point of view, and of his four children, I was *flawed*. Divorced during graduate school, I was his only child with a *failed* marriage. He saw my vulnerability which I believe, ironically, allowed him to be vulnerable with me. And I always did my best to be a nonjudgmental listener.

As my dad told me somewhat awkwardly, he and his young male friends were about twelve years old when they practiced kissing with each other. Their hormones were raging, and they were desperate to explore their sexuality, but deeply afraid to even think about approaching a girl. Catholic doctrine never taught them that same sex sexual experiences were wrong; my father never heard the word homosexual and had no idea that anyone was anything but heterosexual. When he and his fellow lads practiced kissing with each other, it was from a place of innocent curiosity. And since the sexual activity was among boys, they did not regard it as sinful. In their minds, the lads had found a way to explore their sexuality without *going to hell*.

What Larry and his fellow lads experienced might be considered, *situational homosexuality*. The American Psychological Association defines situational homosexuality as *same-sex sexual behavior that develops in a situation or environment in which the opportunity for heterosexual activity is missing and close contact with individuals of the same sex occurs, such as a prison, school, or military setting where individuals are living together, segregated according to their sex. Once away from this setting, the person typically returns to heterosexual activity.*[33] While Larry and his fellow lads lived among girls, for all intent and purposes, they were psychologically separated by institutionalized fear. At the tender age of twelve, they practiced kissing safely, in a same-sex environment. But, as they matured, Larry and his male friends moved into the heterosexual world.

In the summer we had twilight. It would stay light till the wee hours. At about fourteen or fifteen boys and girls from the surroundin' villages met on Sunday night for the Maypole, an outdoor dance. The music was playin' and kids would be dancin' and laughin'. If you liked a girl, you might ask to give her a ride home on the back of your bike. (Larry Cummings)

Although village life was physically and mentally demanding, teenage boys and girls did enjoy a weekly break in the summertime. With the benefit of twilight, the extended day that peaked with the summer solstice in June, it stayed light in Ireland late into the night. Young adolescents took advantage of the evening hour light as dozens gathered from local villages to dance and sing at the outdoor Maypole on Sunday nights.

---

33   https://dictionary.apa.org/situational-homosexuality, 2023.

My father described the Maypole as an outdoor bandstand in the middle of the fields, put on by a local landowner who wanted to make a little extra money. A local farmer who sponsored the event would erect a dance floor, secure entertainment in the form of an accordion, and charge admission. Neither food nor beverages were served. Each participant paid about 6 pence, or pennies, to enter.

The maypole dance got its name from an historic tradition with roots in the Roman Empire, which later found expression among Germanic tribes, and in Great Britain and Ireland.[34] A large wooden pole was erected either in the center of town or the countryside. Often ribbons were attached, and dancers moved circularly around the pole. By the time my dad was a teenager, outdoor dances were still referred to as *Maypoles,* although the setting was a simple dance floor without the traditional center pole. Larry vividly remembers dancing until midnight at the weekend Maypoles with other local village teens who came from a ten-mile radius to meet-up, dance and enjoy the music.

It must have been a welcome relief for young, Irish adolescents to relax and have fun singing, dancing, and socializing each week during the summer months. Without the presence of parents, clergy, and schoolmasters, village adolescents would have enjoyed their unsupervised evenings. Conversely, parents were comforted by the twilight season since sexual activities in village Ireland were connected to darkness. But for the majority of boys and girls, dancing was both the start and end of their village relationships.

Only a handful of young boys and girls would ever marry other local villagers, since land was scarce and non-agricultural work hard to find. In fact, three of every five Irish youths left Ireland

---

34 Wigington, Patti, "A Brief History of the Maypole Dance." *Learn Religions,* June 25, 2019.

during my father's time.³⁵ But the young villagers who attended summer Maypoles didn't think of the dances as opportunities to meet mates; rather, the Maypole was a much-needed release and an opportunity to forge relationships with the opposite sex outside the harsh and punitive world in which adolescents in village Ireland moved into adulthood.

We escaped to the cow houses along the road, where boys and girls would meet up after the dance. But the hens would sit above on the perch and might shit down on yea while we were kissin'. (Lawrence Cummings)

My father's first date was with Maggie McDermott, a fifteen-year-old girl from a village just ten miles away. At age sixteen, my father gave Maggie a ride home from a Maypole on the handlebars of his rusty bicycle. He recalls kissing Maggie in a cow house along the road, a potentially unromantic spot since young lovers were competing for space among farm animals that might *do their business* at inappropriate times. But it was the only private space young villagers had, at least private in the sense that adults were not present. Village adolescents made the most of what was available to them and some inevitably *went too far.*

Johnnie Kelly, Paddy Kilroy, Hud Kelly and I went to a nearby village to meet up with three sisters. Johnnie had seen one of the girls before and he said they were easy with their affections. I was a nervous wreck, but even the fear of God didn't hold me back. I went off into the haystack and we were kissin' and rubbin' each other. I would have met up with them again, but one of my dad's good friends came to see me and told me if I saw those dillies again, he would tell my father. Everyone knew

---

35   Miller, Kerby A. *Emigrants and Exiles.* Oxford University Press, 1988. p. 6.

everyone back then; for miles around, there were no secrets. (Larry Cummings)

All adult villagers regarded the discipline of young people as part of their responsibility. No one would question the authority of a neighbor who reprimanded a village child, even if the discipline included corporal punishment. Values in my father's childhood world were not decisions---they were like the air they breathed or the rain that fell—just the way things were. All villagers shared the same worldview, informed by a small agricultural community with a history of external domination and a strict, punitive version of Catholicism. It was the duty of any villager to *set straight* a young member who was likely to go astray. Small communities hinged on the cooperation of their members, young and old. My father was guided more than once by adult villagers who represented his best interests, defined not by what he as an individual needed, but what the broader community required. Unquestionably, the first line of authority was the Irish Catholic Church.

CHAPTER FIVE:
JESUS, MARY AND JOSEPH AND MY SMALL WORLD

We grew up afraid of God's wrath; there were so many rules. And Ma'am and Dad certainly put the fear of God in us. (Larry Cummings)

During my father's generation, rural Irish Catholicism blended a number of beliefs and traditions that were at once spiritual, superstitious, and culturally driven. Like other Catholic churches it was connected to Rome through an elaborate hierarchy, but local history and customs dominated how villagers interpreted religious teachings. Religion in the Irish countryside in the 1930s had less to do with philosophy and official dogma than behavioral codes. Delivered in concrete terms, the goal was simple---compliance. The result was an intellectual stagnation that did little more than reinforce the status quo. In the end, the very notion of change may have been the gravest sin of all.

Catholicism permeated village life, including visual reminders that hung in every home. In Larry's childhood home, a crucifix hung over both his parents' and grandparents' beds, while the main room featured a picture of Mary, Mother of God. In fact, it was rare for any village home to showcase a decorative picture that did not feature a religious theme.

In addition to visual images, every home would have had at least one set of rosary beads, which would have been blessed by the local priest. Rosary beads were frequently hung on the wall, as they were in my father's home, where they could be easily accessed when *praying the rosary*.[36] But they were also hung for visitors to admire, as rosary beads were frequently the most expensive accessory a village family owned. They were often passed from generation to generation as a valued legacy to be cherished and admired. Rosary beads were frequently given as departing gifts to young Irish adults who were emigrating abroad. The gift of religious beads connected travelers to both their families and their faith. While prayer was centrally important to Irish Catholics, when they looked for comfort and protection they did not look to God or to his son, Jesus.

The Irish prayed to saints who in turn, they believed, communicated with God on their behalf. Known as the *Intercession of the Saints*, the practice dates back to the third century and was formalized at the Council of Trent in 1545 which declared, *the saints who reign together with Christ offer up their own prayer to God for men*.[37] Following the Reformation, Protestants

---

[36] "Praying the Rosary" is a Catholic instrument of prayer and meditation. The purpose is to allow a person to meditate on the mysteries of Christ's life. A Rosary consists of four Mysteries (the Joyful, the Sorrowful, the Glorious, and the Luminous), and each of these Mysteries is broken into five "Decades," with ten beads in each Decade representing an event in the life of Jesus. In addition to beginning and ending with the Sign of the Cross, the prayers include the Apostles' Creed, Our Father, Hail Mary and Glory be to the Father. See Miller, John Desmond, *Beads and Prayers: The Rosary in History and Devotion*. Bloomsbury Publishing, 2002.

[37] Scannell, Thomas. "Intercession (Mediation)." In *The Catholic Encyclopedia*, New York: Robert Appleton Company, 1910.

largely abandoned the practice, but Catholics, particularly Irish Catholics, clung to their belief that the most efficient manner of communicating with God was through a preferred saint. My father followed in his grandmother's footsteps and throughout his life prayed to Saint Anthony. It was only in the world of the sainted that the Irish would take any comfort in their religion.

The rural Irish envisioned God as a strict father figure that punished sinners with all sorts of maladies and sufferings. Even if a person led a God-fearing life, the Heavenly Father might still create misfortune in order to test a person's faith or teach the community a lesson. God had a plan, but it was not the believer's role to discern it.

Irish Catholics, however, might pray to a saint to intervene on their behalf with the Heavenly Father. If prayers were answered, it was because the requestor was deserving. Of course, the Irish were careful with their requests. My father was taught not to be greedy; he would never have asked for material comforts. Among acceptable requests were good health, a good life partner, and fertility in marriage.

Larry recalls that the overwhelming majority of village children did honor the church teachings. Fear was a powerful motivator and a rural Irish upbringing insured that each child got a heavy dose of it. Children felt the fear of burning in hell, the fear of being beaten by an angry parent, and fear of the schoolmaster who similarly carried a rod for corporal punishment. Irish children during my father's time saw the world in terms of black and white, good and bad, Christian and heathen. Every person had to choose either the side of righteousness or the side of damnation.

In addition to the many rules the church laid down, the Irish also regarded certain attitudes as sinful. Pride, for example, was not tolerated. Children were rarely praised since the Irish believed praise might give a child *a big head*. Having an independent voice was also regarded as sinful for a minor. Children were seen and not heard in the presence of adults; to offer an opinion or challenge conventions was blasphemy. Children were expected to adhere to church teachings, protect their personal honor and mind adults. In short, the ideal Irish child was quiet, humble, devout, and chaste.

The long history of Britain's domination over Ireland had created an internalized cultural inferiority complex among many Irish. They expected to suffer and saw harsh treatment as normal. Parents were harsh with their children; teachers with their pupils; and parish priests with their parishioners. The reality of their historic past and current conditions was married with their religious beliefs to produce a monolithic world view where politics, culture and religion were mutually reinforcing.

I was on my way to church with Mike Kelley when we saw the apples hangin' in a neighbor's tree. We had been fastin' since the night before since we were goin receivin' and we were hungry. We couldn't resist takin' a few. But then we were so afraid. If we didn't receive communion at mass, Ma'am would know, and she'd kill me. If I did receive, I would surely burn in hell. I decided the best course was to avoid a beatin' today and worry about the fires of hell tomorrow. Mike Kelly did the same. (Larry Cummings)

All Catholics eligible for communion would have been expected to fast the night before Sunday morning mass. Children were taught that receiving the body and blood of Christ with food in their stomachs was a mortal sin. If a person died with a mortal sin not confessed, he or she would go straight to hell and feel

Satan's fires for all eternity. Hell was not an abstract place for my father and his childhood siblings and friends, but a real physical experience and it was described to them in the most horrific terms.

Mortal sins were contrasted by the Catholic Church with venial sins; if not confessed the former sent you to hell, while the latter merely strained your relationship with God.[38] What constituted a mortal sin during Larry's childhood was less about official church dogma and more about what your community espoused. My father and the other children in the Irish countryside never questioned the categorization of sins. In addition to receiving communion without fasting, village children believed mortal sins included pre-marital sex, murder, and taking the name of the Lord in vain. A full appreciation for the meaning of sin was never explored---even among adults. Children were discouraged---often with physical punishment---from questioning authority figures and rules. As adults, the rural Irish accepted locally understood religious teachings. They did, however, occasionally craft an exception to the strict rules imposed on them.

Many Irish, including my parents and their parents before them, used the phrase *Jesus, Mary and Joseph* when expressing exasperation or frustration. When a parent came upon a child who was misbehaving, or an unattended pot overflowed, or a candle caught fire, both men and women might raise their voices and call out the names of the Holy Family. I asked my dad if that were an instance of *taking the name of the Lord in vain*. He assured me it was not. Rather, Larry insisted it was a manner of praying for patience or resolution to an immediate problem or

---

38 A clear and concise definition of mortal versus venial sins may be located at: https://stboniface-lunenburg.org/mortal-and-venial-sin#:~:text=Mortal%20sins%20are%20grave%20offenses,destroy%20one's%20relationship%20with%20God.

unpleasant situation at hand. While I found his explanation to be more convenient than accurate, I was struck by my father's need to reconcile his behavior with church teachings. Irish Catholicism set a high bar and human behavior had to be reconciled with what must have been an impossible standard.

In his research on Irish Catholicism John Jordan finds consistent themes over time including, an *unreasonable restriction on personal liberty, regimentation, superstition and a disproportionate preoccupation with the morality of carnal sins*.[39] In rural Ireland during my dad's youth Catholicism created a psychological prison of sorts from which there was no escape. And while human life was severely regulated, animal life was not an area of concern.

We had a few cats around the barn to kill the mice and a dog to help round up farm animals. But we couldn't afford to have too many. After a cat or dog gave birth, we'd take the kittens or puppies, put them in a flour bag and drown them in the well. After all, what else was there to do? (Larry Cummings)

Religious practices governed human life and interactions among people and between people and authority figures. Animal life was valued only in its ability to assist human existence. Life in rural Ireland in the 1930s was hard and difficult choices had to be made. Animals may have been pets and a source of comfort and fun for children but first and foremost, they held a functional role. Families living on the verge of subsistence had little to spare and animals were at the end of the pecking order. When they multiplied beyond what a family could use and sustain, they were destroyed. By tasking children with their destruction parents communicated

---

39   Jordan, John. "Irish Catholicism." *The Crane Bag* 7, no. 2 (1983): 106-16.

the harsh realities of life to their offspring at a tender age. Parents believed the sooner a child understood that life was tough and to be endured without complaint, the better.

My father was seven years old the first time he was tasked with drowning kittens. His mother assigned him the task without much sympathy and would not have been tolerant had he refused. Nora placed the kittens and a few stones in a flour sack and handed it to her young son. Larry walked slowly extending the normal ten-minute walk to a nearby abandoned well to nearly twenty minutes as the kittens tumbled inside the sack. He approached the well and slowly opened the bag, reaching in to pat the soon-to-be drowned animal babies. Tears ran down his cheek and Larry thought of releasing the kittens but feared his mother's retribution. After several minutes he tied the top of the sack and dropped it into the well. The young Larry was frozen as he watched the bag descend into the well, listening to the final sounds of the baby kittens. He turned and ran as fast as he could back home, wiping his tears before going into his mother, knowing if he showed weakness, she would chastise him. My father recalls his mother looked at him but never spoke, and a seven-year-old Larry ran immediately to his bedroom where he remained until the next day. He did not come downstairs to eat his dinner and Nora never questioned his loss of appetite. As the Irish were fond of saying, *the less said about it, the better.*

Drowning kittens and puppies never got easier for my dad, and he was relieved when the task was assigned to his younger brother. Even as a senior citizen my father vividly recalled the final sounds and movements in the flour bag as it descended into the water. The sadness in his eyes suggested that even decades later Larry's experiences were still raw.

Nora clearly conveyed to her children that life was difficult and to make it through they needed to toughen up, both physically and emotionally. But she also conveyed the importance of charity and kindness. Irish Catholicism took seriously that everyone was their brother's keeper, and villagers routinely helped each other when illness struck, a baby was born, or a neighbor needed a hand with a new roof for a house or barn. For Nora, Christian charity also extended beyond her village.

The Tinkers came around on a regular basis; Ma'am was always good to them—offerin' them a spot in the barn and some potatoes. Dad used to say they'd burn the place down smokin' their fags. But Ma'am would make them swear they wouldn't smoke in the barn. (Larry Cummings)

Irish Travelers, also known as itinerants, gypsies and tinkers, are a small minority group in Ireland with their own language, beliefs and social customs. Largely marginalized from mainstream society, their origins are still debated among historians.[40] In the 1930s the Travelling People were regarded by rural Irish as the poorest of the poor. Without land and ties to a local church and community, they were at once pitied and feared. Travelers' pattern of land use was frequently at conflict with rural farmers. Although they made up just .5% of the population, in 1939 the Irish Parliament announced it would address itinerancy as it had become *an acute difficulty in rural Ireland*.[41] Charity, however, was also a message that the rural Irish received at mass. No matter how bad things seemed, there was always someone *worse-off*.

---

40 See Sinéad ní Shuinéar, "Apocrypha to canon: Inventing Irish Traveller History." In *History Ireland*. Vol. 12 No. 4 Winter 2004.

41 Helleiner, Jane. "'Menace to the Social Order': Anti-Traveller Discourse in the Irish Parliament 1939-59." *The Canadian Journal of Irish Studies* 24, no. 1 (1998).

My father recalls that the Travelers came around on a fairly regular basis. Although his father was not sympathetic to their pleas for a night's lodging in the barn and a few potatoes, his mother felt differently, especially if a mother and baby were on board. They seemed to come and go quickly, accepting only what was offered with gratitude and then moving on.

Travelers served an important function in the Irish countryside during my father's youth. They reinforced the notion that, poor as village farmers were, their circumstances could be worse. The presence of Travelers reminded local villagers that not only should they accept their material conditions, but they should also be grateful. By offering charity to the Travelers, Irish villagers acknowledged their bounty---meager as it was---and paved the way for their eternal salvation through their good works.

I can recall a few times the priests would take up special collections for the African missions. I 'twasn't at all sure where Africa was or who lived there. We were told their skin was black and they were heathens that needed to be Christianized. Ma'am gave a few pence. (Larry Cummings)

All Irish Catholics were asked from time to time to assist the work of Catholic missions abroad. Of course, young village children who had never traveled more than twenty miles from home had difficulty conceptualizing the far away missions described to them in church. My father had never seen a person of color, but through church teachings he came to understand that Africans were dark-skinned people that lived far away and were in desperate need of Catholicism. Like the Travelers, the story of the heathen Africans served to reinforce the notion that rural Irish were blessed to live in a Catholic world. Wanting anything more than what they had was sinful and might subject them to a life with even less. That they were in a position to give charity—regardless of the amount---meant life was good.

Catholic teachings were reinforced every Sunday at a weekly morning mass where all ages gathered in a small church just over two miles away from my dad's farm. It was the one day of the week where only necessary chores, like milking cows and feeding chickens were performed. Otherwise, the focus was on the Word of the Lord.

Men and women were separated during mass. It wasn't like there was any rule that I knew of, but it was just the way things were. (Larry Cummings)

Church seating reinforced and reflected the reality of gender relations in rural Ireland in the first decades of the twentieth century. Men and boys sat to the right of the church aisle, while women and girls sat to the left. As parishioners listened to the Word of the Lord in Latin--a language they did not understand--they were expected to be in a state of grace. Receiving the sacrament of Penance and fasting before Communion were requirements for Catholics everywhere; but for the Irish, the state of grace meant a purity that could only be achieved through the separation of the sexes. Closeness to God, therefore, depended on a separation from the physical, particularly sexual world. Even to sit side by side in a pew suggested a physical intimacy that Irish Catholics could not brook.

You knew when to sit, to kneel and to stand. You knew when to go receivin' and when to recite your prayers. You listened hard to the priest's homily and then you went on home till next Sunday. (Larry Cummings)

For my father, and undoubtedly for many other young Irish children, Mass was less an exercise in spirituality than an orderly drill. The parish priest conducted the service in Latin, facing the altar with his back to his parishioners. Children quickly learned when to sit, stand, kneel and pray. For as much as an hour each Sunday the parish priest would deliver his homily, the only part of the Mass conducted in English. Homilies reinforced the familiar themes of obedience to God's law, charity and salvation in the world beyond death. For young children, like my father, it was yet another arena—albeit a powerful one---where behavioral codes were reinforced to ensure compliance.

It was a great thing if you had a family member that became a nun or a priest. We had two cousins that became nuns. It was the only thing that earned you braggin' rights. (Larry Cummings)

Although pride was considered sinful among the Irish, they made an exception for the devout who dedicated their lives to the service of God. Having a family member who entered the convent, or the priesthood, earned a family bragging rights and an increased status among local families. In my father's family, two of his uncles had daughters who entered the convent. Certainly, in their eyes it would have been better had the family produced a priest; nonetheless, as far as accomplishments go, the family was delighted to celebrate that two of its women had achieved the pinnacle of female success.

Years later after Larry married and started a family in America, his cousin, Sister Rosetta, would come to visit him and his siblings in the Boston area. She worked in a Catholic orphanage in Texas and visited several times over the course of her life. Each visit was always a course for celebration and *having a nun in the house* gave my father a feeling of great pride.

But as a youth, Larry lived in an insulated space largely defined by Irish Catholicism. For children, like my father, rural Ireland in the 1930s was a small world, a homogeneous and restrictive space, both physically and culturally. For some, education offered a pathway to intellectual enrichment and in a few cases, economic advancement. But, overwhelmingly, the Irish National Schools struggled to provide an elementary education to its populace. Consistent with children's other experiences, elementary schools reinforced harsh discipline and Irish Catholicism.

CHAPTER SIX:
ONE SIZE DOESN'T FIT ALL

They beat us for all sorts of stuff; the worst of it was that you had to cut your own rod. (Larry Cummings)

Village schoolhouses were much like Catholic churches, narrowly focused, stern, rule-laden institutions run by men. Although women did serve as teachers, particularly in the early grades, a male schoolmaster was the norm since it was believed men could provide what children needed most—discipline. After obedience, the national school system also prioritized Catholicism. Although the Irish National Schools were originally founded on the goal to provide non-denominational education, by the late 19th century, the Catholic Church in Ireland controlled the educational system in their parishes.[42]

My father walked to the Ballygar National School for the first time at the age of five, traveling along a dirt road for two miles

---

42   The Irish National Schools were founded in 1831, originally under a non-denominational model. By the end of the century, however, the Roman Catholic Church extended its growing sphere of influence into the educational system, transforming the original model. By the time my father entered the National Schools they were first—and foremost—Roman Catholic schools. See Seamas O Buachalla, *Educational Policy in Twentieth Century Ireland*, Dublin: Wolfhound Press, 1988.

with the other village students, all of whom were barefoot except during the coldest winter months. The path Larry walked was the same road that his father had traveled when he attended the school as one of its first pupils when it opened in 1896. The school served several area villages and students would have come from a ten-mile radius.

Like his father before him, Larry carried a lunch sack that contained soda bread and jam along with a small glass jar filled with milk, fresh from the cow. Unpasteurized, or raw milk, was rich and creamy and my dad loved its taste. But in addition to the much-needed calories it provided children, the likely presence of bacteria would also have caused stomach illnesses, although there is research that supports the benefits of raw milk to children's immune systems.[43] Whatever the cost-benefit, however, raw milk was readily available, and together with bread and jam, it constituted the only lunch village school children would ever know.

The Ballygar School was typical among Irish national schools with a single story, two-room house constructed of stone and concrete and covered with a slate roof. Each room was heated in the winter months by a stove that burned local peat, though my father and his siblings recalled being cold and damp to the core during the winter as stoves were placed next to faculty desks and did little to warm their young students. Comfort was not a consideration when constructing national schools, although they did build two outhouses, one for the girls and another for the boys. Having a private, enclosed spot to go the bathroom was a luxury for the young students in the 1930s and 1940s. Not until 1959 would village students have running water and indoor plumbing

---

43   See, https://www.rawmilkinstitute.org/updates/immunity-the-immune-system-and-raw-milk.

at school.[44] The sparseness of the physical plant was matched in both classroom structure and curriculum.

Each of the two classrooms housed four grades that were divided by rows. The school boasted four teachers and a headmaster. Teachers taught all subjects for their assigned grades, and each child would have the same teacher for two years before moving on to the next level. Educational materials were minimal, and students shared books and writing instruments. There were no microscopes, compasses or scales, although they did have two maps that hung on the wall, one of Ireland and another depicting the globe. The curriculum was basic; students learned to read, write, and do basic math, or *sums* as my dad would say. They also studied history, the Irish language and religion, which permeated the curriculum.

As Larry entered the national school system in the late 1930s, the Catholic Church was the dominant force in shaping education. The Church defended its involvement with the declaration that the *motive in education was the salvation of souls*.[45] To this end, Catholicism was taught both directly and subtly. In addition to catechism class, primary readers, for example, routinely displayed images of families praying the rosary or sitting in mass.[46] Even math could incorporate religion as my dad remembers learning to count using a set of rosary beads. While Ireland's national schools wanted a literate populace, they also insured a strictly Catholic one. From home life to Sunday morning mass, to lessons in school, the messages were mutually reinforcing. Where the national schools

---

[44] Editors: Kelly, B., Kilcommins, P., Lohan, H., and Silke, M. *Rolling Back the Years, 1896-1996.* (The book was published by the editorial committee in celebration of the centennial celebration of the school).
[45] Raftery, Deirdre. "'Among School Children': The Churches, Politics and Irish Schooling, 1830-1930." *Studies: An Irish Quarterly Review* 100, no. 400 (2011): 433-40.
[46] Ibid.

fell short, however, was in their attempt to reinstate Irish as the prevailing language.

With the establishment of the Irish free state in 1922 there was a concerted effort to reinstate Irish as the national language. Both Michael Collins and his rival in the Irish Civil War, Eamon de Valera, stated that the restoration of the Irish language was at least as important as political independence.[47] Ireland's effort to reinstate its native language is consistent with all 19th and 20th century nationalist movements. For example, Greece, Romania, Hungary, Czechoslovakia, Yugoslavia, and Turkey all experienced similar movements. As MacNamara points out:

Linguistic differences were not superficial but derived from deeply rooted distinctive racial characteristics and in turn perpetuated them. To learn and to speak the language of the conqueror was to turn one's back on one's own race, and to enslave one's mind to that of the conqueror.[48]

Like other previously conquered countries, Ireland sought to reclaim its language and culture, and to define itself against its conqueror, Great Britain. As much as Catholicism took center stage among Ireland's educational goals, the Irish language stood right beside it. The national effort to reinstate Irish as the national language began in earnest and continued throughout my father's time in school.

Ireland's educators argued that the most opportune time to introduce Irish was between the ages of six and eight. Teachers' Training Colleges emphasized Irish fluency in their curriculums and special summer courses were designed for existing teachers so

---

47 MacNamara, John. "The Irish Language and Nationalism." *The Crane Bag* 1, no. 2 (1977): 40-44.
48 Ibid. p. 40.

they might turn Irish as a subject into a *medium of instruction*.[49] The goal was to have as many primary teachers as possible speaking fluent Irish throughout the day, and they encouraged their pupils to see Irish fluency as a badge of honor. As Murphy points out, Irish fluency was the only path to being truly Irish. *Along with language the native speaker absorbs a way of thought that is to a certain extent common to all Irishmen, but which finds perfection only in the Irish language itself.*[50]

Efforts to reinstate Irish as the national language greatly increased fluency but did not achieve the desired result.[51] While young students learned Irish as a second language, it never permeated their lives beyond school. There were some spotty rural areas throughout Ireland that had maintained their native tongue, but like most of Ireland, that was not the case in Bornacurra. My grandparents' generation had never spoken anything but English, and since Ireland was still under Great Britain's control, Irish had not been taught to them in school. When their young children came home eager to speak Irish, they quickly were told to return to English. As a consequence, Larry and his siblings learned just a *bit of Irish* as he liked to say.

At family gatherings, my parents, aunts and uncles often had short, superficial conversations in Irish, but they lasted only as briefly as their limited Irish vocabulary allowed. In spite of their Irish language limitations, however, my parents continued to use a few Irish phrases when my siblings and I were growing up. Among their favorites was *Éist do bhéal*, which I always thought was such an eloquent way of being told to shut up.

---

49   Murphy, Gerard. "Irish in Our Schools, 1922-1945." *Studies: An Irish Quarterly Review* 37, no. 148 (1948): 421-28.
50   Ibid. p. 423.
51   Today both Irish and English are the official languages of Ireland.

My father would have his first exposure to Irish in fourth grade where his teacher was fluent and taught all lessons in their native language. He remembers being fascinated and excited about speaking words his parents didn't comprehend. But before the more demanding lessons started, Larry entered what we would characterize today as kindergarten.

Larry's first memories of his entrance into the Irish National Schools are positive, even loving. He recalled a young, sweet teacher who provided a welcoming learning environment for her young pupils. She taught—in two separate rows—the kindergarten, or infant class as it was called, and first grades. Among my dad's early recollections is the graciousness his teacher showed her pupils during the winter months when she gave each a turn standing next to the stove to warm up. But my father's early experience quickly changed from warm and welcoming to stern and punitive as he moved into the second grade.

A matronly woman, who my father recalls as middle-aged, taught both the second and third grades. Since there were not enough chairs to accommodate the students, boys and girls rotated every half-hour. My father would sit for thirty minutes and then stand beside his desk for the next thirty. When standing, he would read his catechism or history books; while seated, he would do his arithmetic or writing assignments using a fountain pen and inkbottle.

It is likely that the disruptive nature of the class fostered an environment that was conducive to talking and disorder among the students. In order to address this, his teacher employed the use of a strap. My father recalls being strapped for talking on more than one occasion. But he was also strapped for incorrectly answering questions.

I was no student; I didn't know the answers half the time. (Larry Cummings)

Larry was not a good student. He struggled in most subjects and was beaten on numerous occasions for his lack of understanding. Larry was, however, a very hard worker on the family farm and his mother routinely kept him home from school to assist her with chores. In fact, the family was cited for truancy by local authorities. As a result, an already struggling student, my father fell even further behind.

My father was certainly not alone in a small farming community where parents kept the *dumb* child home to work on the farm, while insuring the *smart* child attended classes. In my father's family, his brother Mike and his sister Mary, the oldest siblings, were regarded as smart. He and his sister Peggy were not but were both regarded as hard workers, while the others were *middlin* as my dad liked to say.

Larry lived in a time where learning disabilities were unheard of and children were considered smart, dumb or somewhere in between. There were no parent conferences and no report cards. A student was promoted from grade-to-grade or held back, as my father was in third grade. If a child passed his or her exams between fourteen and sixteen years of age, he or she received a Leaving Certificate. This would have been equivalent to a high school diploma, a recognition my father never received.

Larry was grateful when he was able to drop out of school at fourteen years of age, but the emotional scars stayed with him for life. He was both verbally ridiculed and physically beaten by several of his teachers for a period of seven years. He recalls that his worst experience was his final year in sixth grade where his teacher was a stern and forceful headmaster. Here, the abuse was combined; he was strapped while being called *a dummy*. As a consequence, my father was left with a deep insecurity and feeling of unworthiness. He would say that the verbal abuse was harder to take than the physical.

While not every child would have had his experience, unquestionably many did. And those that escaped the strap would still have witnessed the cruelty, since beatings were done in full view of the class. My father recalls that no child would complain to his parents since that would inevitably result in yet another beating.

Corporal punishment was legally tolerated in Irish national schools until 1982. Many of the physical chastisements that were handed out in Larry's day and beyond would easily meet the standards of child abuse today. No serious discussion about the potential adverse impact of corporal punishment on children took place in Ireland until the late 1950s. In addition to the biblical statement, *spare the rod, spoil the child,* the Irish also subscribed to the belief that *a good beating never hurt anyone.*[52] The notion that physical punishment was somehow good for children and would yield positive results encouraged its widespread use. But it may have been that Ireland's National Schools frowned upon teachers administering corporal punishment with a weapon.

My father explained that when inspectors came to visit the school, all rods and straps were tucked away out of sight. This may have been nothing more than tidying up for an inspection, but it may also suggest that even a system that embraced physical punishment had limits on how it would be carried out. Regardless, once an inspector left, sticks and straps quickly reemerged.

---

52 Maguire, Moira J, and Seamas O Cinneide. "'A Good Beating Never Hurt Anyone': The Punishment and Abuse of Children in Twentieth Century Ireland." *Journal of Social History* 38, no. 3 (2005).

Some teachers liked to keep their strap or rod visible as a constant warning to their pupils. But my father also remembers the occasional teacher who sent students outside to cut the very stick that was used to discipline them. Larry actually said that while the process of cutting his own rod was unnerving, he at least he got to select a stick that would deliver the least amount of pain.

Fear may have kept children in order, but it could not transform a student's academic performance. In spite of the many beatings a young Larry received, he struggled academically until the day he left school. In part, it was due to his spotty attendance.

The state regulated the amount of time a child could stay home from the National Schools. It was the local policeman who rode his bike to my father's home to caution his parents that their son, Larry, had exceeded what was allowed by law. If it happened again, they were told, a fine would be imposed. The scare of a financial penalty was enough, and my dad was promptly returned to class.

That the police came out to the Kilcommins home to enforce school attendance was the result of the Irish School Attendance Act passed in 1926.[53] Like many western countries with an extensive rural, farm population, Irish children were often kept home from school in order to participate in farm chores. Similarly, in industrial areas children frequently were put to work rather than attend school. In the late 19th century, Ireland tried to combat *low and irregular* school attendance among its population, but the effort largely failed.[54] That my great-grandmother, Mary Connelly, who was born in 1867 was literate was a point of pride among the family, especially since it was rare for anyone in rural Ireland in

---
53 Fahey, Tony. "State, Family and Compulsory Schooling in Ireland." *The Economic and Social Review*, Vol. 23, No. 4, July 1992, pp. 369-395.
54 Ibid. p. 374.

the 19th century to possess the ability to read and write. But after the formation of the Irish Free State, schools were seen as a *tool of cultural revival,* and the state was willing to use sanctions in using that tool.[55]

The job of enforcing the school attendance act fell to the local police. Headmasters were required by law to turn over attendance records to their area police chief. All children between the ages of six and fourteen were required to attend school without exception. Parents, like the Kilcommins, who tried to side-step the law, as they did when they held my father home to work, received a warning for their first offense. If they did not heed the warning, a fine of 20 shillings was imposed for a second offense, and the fine was doubled for a third offense. The government even maintained the right to remove a child from the home of parents who failed to comply after the third offense. But in the case of Nora and Paddy Kilcommins, one warning was all that was needed, and the police never came to their home regarding truancy again.

Aside from attendance, my dad's recollection is that his parents were not overly interested in the academic performance of their children. He recalls the headmaster coming out to talk to his father about his brother Mike's scholarly potential. But Paddy dismissed the headmaster's plea that Mike should continue his education with the classic retort, *With what? I don't have a pot to piss in or a window to throw it out!*

While the newly formed Irish state did make inroads into education beyond primary school for its youth, the early emphasis was on vocational training. The state's focus for primary education had been the formation of a unified, national identity.

---

55   Ibid. p. 377.

Gifted students, like my Uncle Mike, were unable to convert their educational assets into social mobility in Ireland.[56] As they moved into early adulthood, the overwhelming majority of Irish youth understood their only path forward was to leave their homeland. Paddy and Nora understood the reality of their children's future and accepted it without resistance.

Like most village families, Nora and Paddy lived life in the short run. Day-to-day activities were overwhelming enough; farming, feeding children, cooking and cleaning. They didn't have the luxury of time to contemplate how they might construct a better future for their children, nor did they have the money. Both parents understood that most of their children would leave Ireland for either America or England as they became young adults and would do as generations of Irish had done before them—make it on their own. As a result, Mike was a gifted student who never realized his academic potential in a formal way, and my father would spend the rest of his life believing that hard work was all that he was *cut-out for*.[57]

For my father and his siblings, education was not goal-oriented; there was no sense that you could become anything other than what you were: a poor village kid. It wasn't a path that led you to a better life, rather a contained set of lessons that reinforced what you were and would always be. Not surprisingly,

---

56   Gray, Jane, and Aileen O'Carroll. "Education and Class-Formation in 20th Century Ireland: A Retrospective Qualitative Longitudinal Analysis." *Sociology* 46, no. 4 (2012): 696-711.

57   While he did not pursue education in a formal way, my Uncle Mike Cummings was a political activist and historian. His research focused on Patrick S. Gilmore, known as the "Father of the American Concert Band." Born in Ballygar, Ireland in 1829, Gilmore emigrated to Boston where he made significant contributions to the music world, including writing the lyrics to the song, *When Johnny Comes Marching Home Again*. My uncle's collection of Gilmore-related materials are housed today at the John J. Burns Library at Boston College.

for Larry, the part of school he enjoyed had nothing to do with lessons, but his freedom from them.

My father's favorite part of school was recess, a 30-minute break in the middle of the school day. It was the space where Larry gobbled his jelly and bread and headed out to the fields that surrounded the school. It was here that my dad felt most comfortable. For Irish youth in the countryside, enjoyment was infrequent and appreciated, and while options were limited, opportunities were relished.

CHAPTER SEVEN:
LET'S HAVE A BALL

Sure, I loved it. Most of the time, I'd be the captain. We'd put together a group of lads and play. I was quick and powerful. 'Twas a great feelin. (Larry Cummings)

Larry was not a good student, but on the football field, he felt like a champion. As an athlete, he was strong, forceful and fiercely competitive, and Gaelic football was an arena where my dad could shine. The same lads who witnessed Larry's beatings and inability to get the answers right in class, saw an accomplished authority figure on the field. Weather cooperating, each day at recess the boys would split into two teams and the captains would alternate selecting their teammates. As one of the best players, Larry was frequently captain and took each game seriously, making note of his goals. He recounted with great pride being told by the headmaster that he had a *mean left kick*. That the man who beat him for being a *dummy* also heaped praise on him for his football ability was instructive for my father. He learned that there was more than one way of being successful, and Larry had found his path through physical agility, hard work and determination. Those traits served him well both on and off the football field.

Gaelic football has been played in Ireland for over 700 years. A rough and tumble form of the sport can be traced to the Middle Ages, and eventually it set the foundations for what would become soccer and rugby.[58] By the time my father played, the sport had melded elements of both soccer and rugby and included fifteen players on each team whose physical contact was largely limited to shoulder encounters. In Gaelic football it is illegal to trip, punch, hold, drag, pull or tackle another player. My father had many burned knees and face scratches playing the sport, but he received no serious injuries as a consequence of his frequent matches.

Today, Gaelic football is the most watched sporting event in Ireland. Croke Park, the largest sporting arena in Ireland, is an historic site where the All-Ireland competitions have been held since 1985. Named for Archbishop Thomas Croke, one of the first presidents of the Gaelic Athletic Association (GAA), Croke Park hosted more than 80,000 spectators for the 2019 All-Ireland Gaelic Football Championship.[59]

As a young lad, Larry heard about football championship competitions and he and his friends would walk along local paths cheering, *Up Galway,* before a big game. The nearest team to Larry's home, Galway's Gaelic football team was the local favorite, and although my dad never witnessed a game in person, he was a committed fan. News about wins and losses traveled within days of a meet and had the whole village excited. Like many other children across time and space, Larry likely imagined himself a professional champion when he played football with his local lads.

---

58 See footballgaelique.usliffre.org.
59 Ibid.

In addition to school recess, Larry played football on Sundays after church, and in the summer months, he also played in the evening. Every game was a source of excitement and anticipation with the likelihood of the *big win*. Playing football was the space where my dad felt joy, a sense of happiness and belonging in a world that was often tough and demeaning.

In addition, my father and his fellow lads also played hurling using handmade sticks. Blending elements of football, hockey and golf, hurling is the oldest and fastest field game in the world.[60] Like Gaelic football, hurling continues to draw thousands of spectators in Ireland today. When I returned to Ireland after my father's death, I had the pleasure of watching my son Drew and nephew Larry play the game with their second cousins. My nephew played football in school, and my son played hockey, and they both took to hurling with great ease.

For Larry and his fellow lads, football and hurling were at the center of their social and physical worlds. Wide-open fields were available everywhere in Larry's village, and with handmade sticks and a few balls, there was little cost associated with these popular sports. The passion Larry felt for sports stayed with him well into his adult years.

Years later, after he and his brothers had families in America, they frequently closed a family barbeque with a game of football as their wives, sisters and daughters looked on. As my male cousins grew older, they were often included in the play, but girls were never asked to join in. When Larry was young, games were exclusively a male activity, and my father said it would never have occurred to the boys to include girls, nor were there female teams

---

60   Tom Decen, "*Hurling: the fastest and oldest field sport in the world.*" Sydney Morning Herald, 2015.

that played. Consistent with all aspects of life in rural Ireland in the 1930s and 1940s, sports reinforced gender norms, and girls were excluded.

The brothers carried their belief that football was a male sport into adulthood and would never have thought to include daughters. As time moved on, however, when my siblings and I had families of our own, we too played football after a holiday meal, especially at Thanksgiving. Our games included whoever wanted to play, and one of the best players in our family was my niece, Bonnie, who was an exceptional athlete. Larry embraced playing football with his children and grandchildren, and he took to the field well into his seventies. As an onlooker, I saw joy and excitement resonating from his eyes and I imagine that those games tapped into many happy childhood memories.

Aside from sports, my father does not recall any other type of play. He and his siblings had never been given a single toy as children. For all village children games were something you invented, which required imagination. There was no concept of a Santa Claus that left presents under a tree.

At Christmas, the family gift was the presence of protein on the table in the form of a chicken or ham, which was a rare, and greatly appreciated treat. While the family raised chickens, pigs and cows, surplus animals were sold for much-needed cash, and holding onto meat for their own table was a rare occurrence. My grandmother did hang Christmas stockings for her children and a piece of fruit was placed in each one. Having a special meal served on the occasion of Jesus' birth was a grand celebration, but limited space at the table meant the younger children ate on the floor. The culmination of the grand day, following mass and a special Christmas dinner, was a sweet cake. Even as a senior, my father's eyes lit up when he described the Christmas holiday, as Christmas was the only time each year he would enjoy cake.

Birthday cake and celebrations did not exist in Larry's world. No child had his or her birthday celebrated in the rural villages of Ireland during my father's time. The very thought would have been laughable. Multiple children in village families was the norm, and hardly a cause for annual celebration. The very thought of making a child feel special was anathema to rural Irish values. But for some lucky children, there was the occasional opportunity to get outside their narrow world and take a peek into what life might be like elsewhere.

I saw just one picture show growin' up—it was an American film with John Wayne. We thought America must be a grand place. (Larry Cummings)

There were movie houses in Irish cities during the 1940s, but few villagers could afford the luxury on any regular basis. There was also the sense among the clergy and many parents that movies might perpetuate values that were not consistent with Catholic teachings.[61] But after earning his own money working for a local farmer after school, Larry was allowed to go into town and see the first and only movie he would ever see in Ireland. My dad walked eleven miles into Roscommon town with another local lad and vividly remembered the thrill of sitting in the movie house as the electric lights were dimmed and the projector started. He was in awe every minute as the John Wayne western played on the screen, which gave Larry his first look at America.

Childhood dreams for many Irish children centered on a future across the pond, where jobs abounded, and even ordinary

---

61 Eds. "Ireland in the 1930s and 1940s". *Muckross House Research Library*, Killarney, Co. Kerry, Ireland.

people had bathrooms and electricity. My father's impressions of America primarily came from his uncles who wrote to their brother Paddy Kilcommins on a regular basis. Paddy must have missed the brothers he left behind when he returned to Ireland, and it is likely that while he enjoyed hearing the news from America, the letters also provoked feelings of sadness.

Once in America, Irish immigrants were called *Yanks* by the Irish at home. Larry remembers his father going into the local post office and returning to announce, *there is news from the Yanks*. Nora would be more interested in what might have been in the letter since the brothers often enclosed a few dollars, especially at Christmas. But the older children would gather around their dad and listen to the latest news. In the early 1940s, the news was primarily about the war.

Families in rural Ireland were physically and mentally distant from the events of World War II. Ireland declared neutrality after Germany invaded Poland in 1939, and officially referred to the war as *The Emergency*. In spite of pressure from England, and later from the United States when it entered the war in 1941, Ireland maintained its neutrality.[62] Fewer than 5% of the country had access to radio transmissions during my father's youth, so news about the war was spotty, and likely not always up-to-date and accurate.[63] As a consequence, the world altering events of World War II had little impact on rural Ireland.

This is not to suggest it was a non-event in Ireland, however. In the initial years of the war when the outcome was not determined, debates raged about which side would better benefit Ireland. The

---

[62] White, Timothy J., and Andrew J. Riley. "Irish Neutrality in World War II: A Review Essay." *Irish Studies in International Affairs* 19 (2008): 143-50.

[63] Eds. "Ireland in the 1930s and 1940s". *Muckross House Research Library, Killarney, Co. Kerry, Ireland.*

Irish Republican Army (IRA), an illegal paramilitary organization which lost the Civil War and refused to recognize Northern Ireland or the Irish Free State, covertly worked with German intelligence in the hopes victory might lead to a united Ireland. But Germany also bombed Dublin as a warning when it appeared the government's negotiations with the Great Britain might lead to Ireland's abandonment of its neutrality policy.[64]

There were Irish who volunteered for the British army in support of the Allied war effort. While historians debate the exact number, 28,000 is a conservatively accepted estimate. Many of the Irish volunteers were already working in England and were given the choice between returning to Ireland or accepting eligibility for conscription.[65] For those who chose to serve, no doubt the financial compensation was an incentive, since jobs were scarce at home. For others, volunteering for the British army may have been a quest for adventure. But, overwhelmingly, the Irish supported the Allied war efforts.

My father recounted his schoolteachers telling their classes about the war and they universally sided with the Allies. In spite of Irish animosity toward Great Britain, all Irish in the countryside had relatives in England and America who wholeheartedly supported their new homeland; and, in turn, their families in Ireland supported them. Larry left school as the war was ending with little understanding of its global consequences.

Not unlike the Depression, World War II was a major global event that did not alter the day-to-day routines of rural Ireland.

---

64 White and Riley, 2008. In addition, see Dublin City online history and photographs of the bombing at: https://www.dublincity.ie/library/blog/north-strand-bombing-80thanniversary#:~:text=The%20North%20Strand%20Bombing%20occurred,the%20destruction%20of%20300%20houses.
65 Girvin, Brian, and Geoffrey Roberts. "The Forgotten Volunteers of World War II." *History Ireland* 6, no. 1 (1998): 46-51.

Supply chains were certainly interrupted, but life for subsistence farmers changed little. Larry and his friends continued on with their daily diets of largely potatoes and root vegetables, and with their farming work and football games in the fields. As a young adolescent, Larry had little interest in anything that didn't impact him directly. That was not true of my grandfather.

My dad recalls his father reading American newspapers and magazines that were sent to him by his brothers in America. He seemed to gobble up everything that arrived by mail, regardless of how out-of-date. Undoubtedly, he and his colleagues at work would have discussed the war and its global implications. Intellectually curious, Paddy was grateful for any opportunity to read about current events since access to materials in rural Ireland were nonexistent.

My father's family and the other villagers did not have access to a library. The closest library to Bornacurra was in Galway, more than 50 miles away. For today's students, where information is a google search away, this is incomprehensible. But, when knowledge was information written and published for readers who had access to bookstores, newsstands and libraries, intellectual subjugation was a fact of life in rural Ireland. For my grandfather, a bright, avid reader, newspapers, magazines and the occasional book from America made all the difference in a rural world where intellectual curiosity could not be easily satisfied.

For young Larry, however, it was a world he embraced, and unlike many of his peers, he did not want to leave his homeland. He loved farm life and believed he might take over *the place* someday. With the war's end, his eldest sibling, Mike was working on emigrating to America. His brother John was also discussing the potential, as were his two sisters. While it was still customary for one of the sons to take over the family farm and take care of elderly parents, the responsibility no longer fell exclusively to the oldest son. Paddy Kilcommins recognized his son Mike's intellectual curiosity and encouraged him to go to America. It is also likely he did not want his son to make the ultimate sacrifice he made when he returned home from America. Paddy wrote to his brothers who agreed to sponsor my uncle and provide him with a home until he could get established.

Paddy, like other village parents, understood that their children would grow up and leave for opportunities abroad. For so many Irish, Ireland was a purgatory of sorts—the place you waited until the gate of America's heaven opened. But this was not the case for Larry who very much wanted to remain in his homeland.

My dad and I discussed at length his desire to remain in a world that seemed to me to be more than impoverished, but also insulated and uninteresting. As a child and young adult, my father never saw a city; in fact, he left Ireland for England having never been more than 15 miles from his home. Although children saw maps at school and read letters from former villagers abroad in England and America, they had no context in which to interpret what they saw or read. Imagination is highly personal and for village adolescents, like my father, each must have constructed what life abroad was like through the lens of his or her own experiences.

In spite of the harsh realities of life, my father recalls having fun, experiencing the feeling of joy from time-to-time. He loved to farm and was good at it, and his daily productivity fed his self-esteem, which was reinforced by his mother. Nora came to depend on my dad for the majority of farm work, so it seemed reasonable that Larry would anticipate remaining in Bornacurra. And while he loved farming, it is also likely Larry embraced his rural life in Ireland because he had never experienced anything else.

Today's children are exposed to what they don't have, so they understand that there are *haves* and *have-nots*. With access to global information, a child quickly learns where he or she stands in relationship not only to local peers, but also to the broader society. With easy access to social media, today's adolescents are inundated with material culture whether they can afford it nor not. Larry understood that there were *rich people* in the world, but they were a distant concept, not a reality that he confronted on a daily basis.

In addition, my dad described his world after he left school as *stress free*. There were no terrorists or natural disasters to watch on television. Everyone you knew lived as you did and shared the same values. Life was predictable and safe, and for my dad, that was enough. Larry's wants were few: farm work, enough food to eat, and some fun on the fields playing football with the lads and the occasional dance with the girls. But Larry's dream of taking over the family farm ended the night he confronted his father for abusing his mother.

CHAPTER EIGHT:
AND THEN THERE WERE TWO

Ma'am had worked hard all day in the fields. Dad came home after a couple pints and threw the pan across the room at my mother because his dinner was cold. I clocked him on the spot and told him if he ever hurt my mother again, I'd kill him. That was the end of that. (Larry Cummings)

My father was a grown, young man of 19 years on that fateful day that he struck his father for the first and last time. At the age of 14, Larry had been thrilled to leave school behind, and the ridicule and physical punishment that accompanied it. He settled into life as a hard-working farmer who made extra money cutting peat in the local bogs while enjoying football games with his lads, and dances with the local ladies. As the hardest worker among his siblings, my father believed he would marry a local girl and carry on the Kilcommins name and farming tradition in Ballygar. But his world came to an end the night he physically challenged his father, not as a young boy, but as a man. His older brothers were already in America, leaving my father to fill a senior position in the family.

My father never recalled his father abusing his mother before that fateful night. Perhaps it was a singular event, or perhaps he simply had never witnessed it. That a man had the right to discipline his wife would have been accepted in my father's world. In a gendered society where women were at once essential and yet devalued, no one would have felt sympathy for his mother. Nora was known as a tough woman with her own opinions. And, while feminine strength was a positive virtue during childbirth, farming, cooking, and cleaning, it was not when it came to standing up to a man.

Not until 1996 would Ireland pass comprehensive legislation outlawing domestic violence.[66] During the 1950s when my dad was a young man, no one would have thought twice about a man who physically disciplined his wife. Historian Erin Lambert has argued that the Catholic Church also perpetuated a hostile climate within gender relationships through misogynistic doctrines that inevitably tainted many aspects of Ireland's social, political and legal systems.[67]

Misogyny is certainly borne out in the Irish Constitution which was drafted in 1937 and included a ban on divorce. The ban was lifted by amendment at roughly the same time domestic violence was outlawed. But Irish sentiment which promoted rights for women did not exist in the early 1950s when Nora experienced abuse at her husband's hands. For Nora, her only option was to stay silent and take her husband's assault. But Larry would not accept such treatment for his mother.

---

[66] An excellent summary of the Domestic Violence Bill, 1996 is found in Canavan, John and Coen, Liam's *"Domestic Violence in Ireland: An Overview of National Strategic Policy and Relevant International Literature on Prevention and Intervention Initiatives in Service Provision*, National University of Ireland, Galway. January 2008.

[67] Lambert, Erin K. "Origins of domestic violence in Ireland: an historical perspective." *Canadian Woman Studies*, vol. 17, no. 3, summer-fall 1997, pp. 16-19.

My father absolutely adored his mother, and witnessed her consistently hard work, day-in and day-out. They worked the fields side by side for years while his father worked at his desk job and was frequently out socializing without his wife. My dad recounted stories to me of his mother nursing his youngest sibling Paddy in the fields, placing him back in a homemade carry-sack, and then returning to her field work. Such stories were typical when he discussed Nora. I cannot recall a single time when my father talked about his childhood that he was critical of his mother. This was not the case with his father.

Larry came to see his father as a bad husband and father, a selfish man who gave no credit to his hard-working wife, assigned parental duties to his oldest son, and frequently socialized without his wife. While Larry could appreciate that the men of the village would gather at the pub for a pint, he thought it was wrong of his father to go off to a wedding or wake without his mother. Moreover, since Paddy traveled throughout Galway for his work, he met fellow Irishmen from a number of villages. As a result, he became an unofficial matchmaker, setting up couples for marriage. Arrangements were often discussed at a family's dinner table where again, Paddy would accept an invitation and go alone. It may have been Nora complained to my dad, or perhaps he just perceived her loneliness. But Larry blamed his father for what he saw as his mother's plight. Larry's siblings, however, did not consistently share his assessment.

My late Aunt Mary, the oldest daughter, recalls that her father was intelligent, thoughtful, and while tough on her and her sister, Paddy could be loving and fun. While she acknowledged he used corporal punishment with his children, she claims he never abused their mother. Apart from my father, Mary viewed her mother as often difficult and demanding, a woman who frequently seemed to enjoy *stirring the pot.* Her father, she said, often ignored Nora's tendency to *carry on,* and was often dismissive of his wife. But she insisted it didn't go beyond that.

Similarly, my late Uncle Mike had a positive relationship with my grandfather. Both men preferred intellectual pursuits to farming, and after Mike left Ireland, the two men frequently corresponded through letters discussing politics and life in America. Mike understood that he was the closest to his father and said that Paddy possessed patience and calibrated his emotions. He suggested that the event between my dad and grandfather may have been an overreaction on Larry's side. Perhaps, he speculated, Paddy threw the plate down on the floor and not at his wife.

My Aunt Peg also remembers a kinder relationship with her father. Like Mike and Mary, she recalls a thoughtful, caring man who provided for his family through his work on the County Council. That he even had such a job, she said, was a credit to his intelligence and work ethic. My aunt confirmed, however, that my father was much more *his mother's son, than his father's.* Larry identified with his mother's commitment to the family farm, and he supported her whole heartedly.

When Paddy—likely influenced by alcohol—threw a pan, hitting Nora and yelling that his meal was cold, my father erupted. Larry would not allow anyone to hurt the mother he loved, respected and admired. His attack on his father was immediate and decisive, throwing a punch that landed Paddy Kilcommins on the floor. And that moment sealed Larry's fate.

My grandfather didn't retaliate in the moment, and I suspect he would have been afraid to do so. My father was a strong, forceful figure as a young adult, and he was totally devoted to his mother. My grandfather went to his room, saying nothing to his insubordinate son.

Later, Paddy Kilcommins turned to his children's surrogate parent, his eldest son Mike, to resolve the issue. Although he was in America, my grandfather wrote to his oldest son, and assigned him the task of telling my father he had to go. More than two years went by, and nothing was said of the altercation until Mike returned to Ireland, and in a face-to-face meeting informed my father there was *no room for him* at home.

Mike explained to Larry that he had done wrong by attacking their father, regardless of what he did to their mother. Mike was not interested in sorting out versions of the story; in his eyes Larry was wrong and he told my father he should leave the house immediately. Their father had tolerated his presence the last two years but would do so no longer. My grandfather was not the kind to forgive and forget and was clearly too intimidated by my father to give the order directly. He likely also knew his wife was on their son Larry's side. Not surprisingly, Larry did not challenge his brother Mike.

Larry's oldest male sibling was the epitome of perfection in my father's eyes. Tall, handsome, intelligent—or *book smart* as my father used to say—religious, responsible and respectful of his elders, Mike held his younger brother's admiration and respect. Mike had *checked* his younger brother Larry many times over the course of their childhoods and represented the foremost authority figure in my father's life. Where Larry often regarded his father as wanting, not living up to his family responsibilities, Mike was the closest version of familial strength and integrity that my father could imagine. That Mike returned to Ireland at his father's request says much about his sense of duty and responsibility and his place in the family. While my father angrily challenged his father when he assaulted my grandmother, he would never have challenged Mike. Larry was told to leave by his eldest brother, and while he knew he had to obey, he was at a loss for where he should go.

For young farmers, like Larry, there were few opportunities in Ireland during the 1950s. Known as the *Decade of Doom and Gloom,* unemployment was high and national economic growth low.[68] Fully 16% of Ireland's population, overwhelmingly young adults, emigrated during the decade.[69] Widespread emigration was the inevitable result of the Irish state's failure to modernize agriculture, or encourage non-agricultural employment for its youth.[70]

With no opportunities in his homeland to do the only work Larry believed he *was cut out for,* the now nearly 21-year-old farmer was at a complete loss. He recalls Mike's return visit home as the lowest time in his life. Larry felt rejected, depressed and terribly anxious about what his future might hold. Although he had family in America, Larry lacked the funds needed to get there.

Unlike his older siblings, including Mary, John and Peg, who had planned to go to America and had saved their passages, my father was ill-prepared to depart for a new life across the pond. Extra money he had made working for area farmers, cutting peat in the bogs, was surrendered to his mother. Larry hadn't saved money to emigrate because he never imagined doing so. Unlike his siblings, he had no desire to leave. Larry loved farming, adored his mother and wanted to remain on running the family

---

68 Ó Gráda, Cormac. *A Rocky Road: The Irish Economy Since the 1920s.* Manchester, Manchester University Press, 1997.
69 Ibid.
70 Delaney, Enda. *Demography, State and Society: Irish Immigration to Britain, 1921-1971.* Liverpool University Press, 2000.

farm. My father believed he would do as generations before him had done, marry an Irish girl, have a family and provide for his elderly parents.

With no thought of where he might go, Mike suggested my dad should go to England. Immigration to England was easy for Irish workers as no visas were required.[71] Mike helped my dad get a passport and through conversations with other villagers, Larry learned there was another lad who was going by boat across the Irish Sea to England. They could work on the boat so they wouldn't have to pay passage, and once in England, they would head to Manchester where many Irish settled, and work was plentiful. In the two weeks that Mike visited, my dad's future came to an end, and he had developed a precarious exit plan.

Larry recalls his father mostly avoided him during Mike's visit. The two men never discussed the order my dad received to leave home. As the Irish saying went, *the less said about it, the better*. And Paddy wanted his defiant son gone, without discussion. But his mother was devastated that her husband had written to Mike without her knowledge and ordered her hardest working and most devoted child to leave.

The night before my dad left his mother helped him tie up his few clothes in a flour sack, and with tears pouring down her face, she handed my dad a pound note. Today, that note would be worth about $30.[72] It was from the monies Larry had given his mother over the years since he had left school and picked up extra work in the bogs. My dad told my mother he didn't want it, that she should keep it, but Nora insisted. *You'll need a bit until you get somethin'*, she told him. And the next morning, with his flour

---

71   Ibid.
72   2023 exchange rate.

sack and a pound note, Larry kissed his crying mother goodbye and headed to the Irish Sea.

It took the two lads three days to get to the coast of the Irish Sea in Dublin and locate the boat that would take them to England. For the most part, they walked, though there were a few kind farmers along the roads that offered them rides in their horse-drawn carts. They were grateful for the kindness of families along the way that let them sleep in their barns and offered them bread and jam. Like the Travelers my dad called Tinkers who came to his farm in his youth, my dad was similarly dependent on personal charity.

In Dublin, the two lads worked at the dock loading a freight boat in exchange for a ride across the Irish Sea to Liverpool, a journey that took a full day. The boat was cramped and dirty and my father who had never seen a sea was in awe of the waves and remembers loving the sea breeze. Like the overwhelming majority of Irish, he was a non-swimmer and when I asked if he had access to a lifejacket, he laughed. *Sure Kathy,* he said, *if there'd been a bad storm I'd be goin' to heaven by way of the Irish Sea.*

My father and his fellow traveling companion arrived in Liverpool with enough money to board a train to Manchester where they would start a new life. My dad's companion was fortunate in that he had family in Manchester who welcomed him, housing him until he could launch an independent life. As a result, he and my father went their separate ways after their arrival. But Larry had to make it on his own when he arrived in Manchester, and his transition to a new urban world proved frightening and isolating.

Within just a few days, my father who had never been on any mode of transportation other than a bicycle or horse-drawn carriage had boarded a ship and then a train. Larry felt terribly depressed when he got to England since he was unsure if he would ever see his homeland and mother again. But more than sadness, he felt fear because everything was new and different.

My father and I discussed his arrival in England many times. At first, he would admit that he was a *bit nervous*. But I could see he was holding back, and with encouragement my dad held back a tear and told me, *Jesus, I was terrified*. Larry was encountering a scary, foreign world with no family or friends, and he was uncertain just how he would make out. What my father didn't know was that back at home his younger brother was also overwhelmingly sad, but for very different reasons.

My Uncle Paddy recalls a deep sense of loss when my father left the family home. Mike had departed in 1947 when Paddy was only nine. Mary left two years later, and John and Peg, who left in tandem, followed in 1950. As the Kilcommins family home emptied, Nora struggled to maintain the farm, especially as she got older. My father had been her rock, and there can be no doubt she deeply missed her son's hard work, the extra money he brought in, but perhaps most of all, his devotion. My father's departure left just Tom and Paddy at home. In just a few years' time, Nora's brood had been reduced to two. And it wouldn't be long before Tom departed for America as well. Irish village traditions still mandated that one child would remain to manage the family farm and look after aging parents. My father's departure, and later Tom's, meant that Paddy would have to carry on the family farm, something he never wanted. It was his dream to go to America. But the fight between my father and grandfather had lasting consequences for the two brothers. Larry lost his dream of running the family farm, and Paddy lost his dream of leaving it.

CHAPTER NINE:
SAINT ANTHONY HELP ME–I WASN'T READY FOR THIS

My father arrived in England as an innocent 21-year-old man, unaware what a world-class city like Manchester might hold for him in 1953. For many Irish of his time, Manchester was the chosen destination when migrating to England. As the first industrialized city in the western world, Manchester had long been established as a city where the Irish could find work. Irish migration to Manchester began in earnest in the 19th century and by 1850 fully 10% of the city's population was Irish. Recent immigrants tended to live together in a section of the city that became known as *Little Ireland*.[73]

Ill-prepared for city living, the Irish took any job they could find, and often found themselves in cramped, dirty slums. While conditions had improved by my father's time, relative to the English, the Irish still inhabited slum-like conditions. This was especially true for new arrivals. My father's first home abroad was

---

[73] See "A History of Little Ireland," p.1 http://www.prideofmanchester.com/mancirish/history1.htm.

a sparse, frequently dirty, and smelly rooming house. It was the least expensive housing Larry could find.

Same-sex rooming houses were common in industrialized cities since the 19th century. When my father arrived in Manchester during the early 1950s, both rooming and boarding houses were widely available. In addition to a bedroom, boarding houses often served meals, and a few also provided laundry services. Rooming houses, however, provided only a room to sleep and gave tenants access to shared kitchen and bathroom. As the least expensive alternative, it was my father's choice.

The rooming house Larry called home upon his arrival in England contained twelve private rooms, each with a lock on the door. Larry's bedroom was small and narrow with a simple cot and a three-drawer bureau. There were a few hooks along the peeling walls to hang clothing. At the end of the hall there was an open, single toilet. While Larry had never enjoyed indoor plumbing, he found his new toilet repulsive, since it was rarely cleaned and always smelled.

The small utility kitchen wasn't much better. Before making a meal, which for Larry was usually eggs and potatoes, he took the sole, always filthy pan outside to clean it. My dad used dirt and small stones to scrub the pan prior to cooking. When I asked how he cleaned a pan using dirt, which seemed counterintuitive to me, my dad demonstrated by taking a pan off his kitchen stove and bringing it outside to his backyard. He proceeded to scrub the pan with a rag, some water, dirt and small stones and to my amazement, the pan was immaculate in about ten minutes. *Kathy, my dad said, there wasn't always chemicals for cleanin' ya know.* While the common spaces may not have been clean, they were filled with people from my father's homeland.

Larry explained that the rooming house was rented to Irish immigrant men of various ages. A few, like Larry, were younger and staying at the house in order to earn enough money to get to America. Others, he said, had fallen on *hard times,* and struggled with addiction issues and the loss of families. My dad recalled having little interaction with his fellow boarders other than the perfunctory *good mornin'* or *goodnight.* Turnover, Larry explained, was high since the house boarded on a week-to-week basis. As a consequence, it did not provide my father with a sense of community.[74] It was another unsettling aspect of Larry's new life in an uncertain world.

Jesus, I had never seen a Black person before. I followed the first Black man I saw around nearly the day. (Larry Cummings)

My father had lived in a small, rural, and homogeneous world and, within a 24-hour journey, found himself in a large, urban and diverse city. Although he was in his early twenties, everyone Larry had ever seen before emigrating to Manchester had been white, Irish Catholics. He had never encountered an individual that wasn't of his own race and faith. When my father saw a man with black skin in Manchester he was stricken. He had been taught in church that Black people lived in Africa and wanted very much to become Catholics. Now he was in Manchester and saw a man with black skin and, as he followed him, he saw the man did the same things that he did. The man with black skin went to work, bought food and smoked the occasional cigarette. Larry was beginning to come to terms with global realities and modernity as

---

[74] Although her work focuses on Leicester, Maye-Banbury has an excellent study on Irish rooming houses during my father's time. See, Maye-Banbury, A. (2017) 'Strangers in the Shadows - An Exploration of the 'Irish Boarding Houses' in 1950s Leicester as Heterotopic Spaces'. *Irish Geography,* 51(1), 115-136.

he gradually began to leave behind a world view crafted by a rural, Irish-Catholic upbringing.

Everything about Manchester was foreign to Larry: cars, buses, traffic patterns, urban crime, and a dense and diverse population. My father found it all unsettling, and he admitted, quite frightening. He met an older Irishman who cautioned him about pickpockets and explained thieves often targeted rooming houses where they expected innocent newcomers might leave money. He was advised to never leave money in his room, carrying just what he needed to buy food and depositing the rest on payday in the local bank. Larry had come from a world where the worst crime he knew was young children stealing apples off a tree. That anyone would steal from a hardworking man was shocking to my dad. But before Larry had to worry about protecting his money, he had to earn some. The pound note he had been given by his mother was quickly gone after he bought a train ticket, a little food, and paid a deposit to the rooming house. Larry had to put his fears aside and he looked to his fellow Irishmen in Manchester who told him where to go to find work.

Like so many other Irish, my father sought work as a laborer at one of the oldest and most successful construction companies in the United Kingdom, Wimpey. Named for its founder, George Wimpey, the company was founded in 1880 and was a giant by the time my father arrived in Manchester in the 1950s. After World War II, Wimpey had returned to building homes for private sale.[75] My father eagerly accepted a position as a laborer and soon was acknowledged for his strong work ethic.

---

75   For a complete history of Wimpey, see the corporate site: https://www.taylorwimpey.co.uk/about-us/who-we-are/our-history#na.

There was a group of us lads they tried out for a week. But they let a few of the lads go but kept me on. I thanked the boss, and he said "Don't thank me. I didn't keep ya on 'cause I like ya, I kept ya on 'cause you're the hardest worker of the lot." (Larry Cummings)

My father always beamed with pride when he recounted that story. That insecure lad who was ridiculed in school had always found pride in his ability to stand out for his work ethic. That Larry was chosen above a number of laborers gave him a sense of self-worth, and for the remainder of his life, his strong work ethic defined him. It would always be who Larry was, what he was good at, and his source of confidence. But in so many other ways, my father's insecurities were always evident.

After I got a job and got paid, I wanted to send money to Ma'am. I put it in an envelope with her name and village and tossed it into what I thought was a postbox. Turned out the damned thing was a dumpster. (Larry Cummings)

The Irish were socialized to be humble, and to deflect attention from themselves. My father was quite proud when after a couple weeks on the job he was able to send a pound note home to his mother. Larry learned that postboxes were red-colored and all he needed to do was drop his addressed, stamped letter in the box. My dad located a reddish, large box at the corner of his street, lifted the lid and proudly dropped his letter addressed to his mother with a pound note enclosed. Days later when he observed trash being placed in the box, Larry asked a coworker why trash was being dumped into a postbox. *That is no postbox*, his coworker replied, *it is a skip*.[76]

---

76   Skips are what Americans call dumpsters. For a history of the evolution of the word see: https://enviroskiphire.co.uk/2023/01/history-of-the-skip-what-to-know/#:~:text=The%20 term%20'skip'%20is%20derived,1940s%20in%20the%20United%20Kingdom.

Larry was devastated that he had lost half a week's pay through his ignorance. My father's weekly pay, which he received in English currency, would have been equivalent to about $9.00 in U.S. funds. Eager to make extra money, Larry worked any additional hours offered to him and picked up any side job that he could find. Routinely, Larry *picked up a few extra bucks each week*. But every pound was hard-earned and the loss of his wages, intended to help his mother, was a painful blow to my dad.

Larry might have asked someone to show him where the postbox was located and exactly how to post a letter home, but he would not. To ask for help would reveal ignorance and draw attention, something he couldn't brook. While he eagerly accepted information and advice that were offered, he did not ask how to perform mundane tasks in his new urban environment.

Similarly, my Uncle Mike left Ireland aboard a flight to America, and as his first flight, he was unfamiliar with protocols and procedures. When the flight attendant offered him the complimentary airline meal, he refused, suspecting he might have to pay for it. Although he was quite hungry, he didn't want to spend what little money he had. Mike would never have asked the flight attendant if the meal were included in the fare since this would show ignorance and draw attention. In the same way, my father wouldn't ask exactly how to post a letter. After tossing his hard-earned wages into a local dumpster, through observation, Larry soon learned how to correctly mail his mother a portion of his wages each month.

No doubt Nora received her son's contribution to her family's economy with mixed feelings. Every little bit helped, and she would have been happy to put my dad's monetary gifts to good use. But each envelope would have also been a reminder of the loss of her hardest worker and greatest champion. Nora would have known that my dad was barely getting by, but still found a way to send her a little something each pay day.

My father told me he worked as much as possible and accepted any offer of overtime. To conserve every penny possible, Larry did not pursue a social life and spent no money at bars, movie houses, or any form of entertainment. His one *treat* was the occasional cigarette, which could be purchased as singles and Larry smoked one or two each week. Staying apart from the social milieu in Manchester was first-and-foremost about saving money, but fear was also a factor.

I saw these gals walkin' up and down the street wearin' lip stick and tight dresses. One of the Irish, older guys told me they were prostitutes. What the hell is a prostitute? I asked. (Larry Cummings)

Urban realities frightened my father, and he felt alone in a foreign world. Larry's strategy was to keep his head down, work hard, save his money, send what he could to his mother, and get to America as soon as possible. Larry knew if he just *kept at it* he would get to Boston. My father described to me what today we would see as signs of depression and anxiety. He talked about stomach aches, headaches, and difficulty sleeping while in England. No doubt an overwhelming sense of loneliness contributed to his mental state.

My dad's sole comfort came from attending weekly mass. With a significant Catholic population, Larry had no trouble finding a Catholic church in Manchester. It was at mass where he embraced the comfort of home and as he knelt to pray, the words in his head were always the same, *Please Saint Anthony let me get safely to*

America. There, he would have family, friends and the comfort of his connections to home.

My father absolutely believed that it was Saint Anthony who watched over him and kept him safe in England. His faith was unwavering, and the solace he found in church was a lifeline during a fearful and lonely time in his life. He kept telling himself it was all temporary because soon he would get to America.

But to get there, Larry had a list of necessities. First, he would need the cost of an airline ticket from England to New York and on to Boston. International air travel was 40% more expensive in the 1950s than today, and it was no small achievement to save for a flight to America.[77] Once he saved the cost of a one-way flight, Larry needed to purchase what he labeled a *proper* suit of clothing, a change of shirts, dress shoes, and every-day clothes as well as a suitcase to put them in. There were second-hand stores in Manchester, and it was in one such shop that my dad bought his first suitcase, and although it was used, it was a significant improvement over the flour sack that held his meager belongings when he arrived in England. But for his suit, Larry very much wanted it to be new.

It was important to my dad that he arrive in America looking, as he said, *respectable*. International air travel was an exciting luxury in the 1950s and Larry wanted to look the part. While today, comfortable and casual define air travel apparel, in the 1950s travelers often wore their best, and men were generally in jackets and ties while women wore dresses or suits, frequently accompanied by pearls.[78] My father wanted to wear a new suit on

---

77 Brownlee, John. "What It Was Really Like to Fly During the Golden Age of Travel." *Terminal Velocity*, December 5, 2013.
78 Ibid.

the plane, not only to conform to dress expectations, but to send a message to his siblings, particularly to his brother Mike, when he arrived in America.

Before my dad departed from the family home in Bornacurra, his brother Mike had written his American address on a sheet of paper and told my father to keep it with him. Once settled, Larry was to write his brother with word of his employment and residence. If—and when—my dad saved the necessary monies needed to travel to America, Mike would arrange sponsors and facilitate my dad's immigration. Mike's words to my father made it clear that he was not overly confident his younger brother would make it. Mike knew my dad was not a good student and his only skill was farm labor. As he departed for Manchester, Mike wondered how Larry would get on, much less save enough money to get to Boston.

My father was determined to get off the plane in Boston looking *proper* in front of his brother and the world. In addition to his travel money, my dad saved enough to buy a new suit, which was a momentous occasion in his life. Not since his cousin Anthony died, leaving a seven-year-old Larry the beneficiary of his clothing, did my dad have store-bought clothing. On his day off, Larry walked to the *fancy part* of the city where he was fitted for a new suit. It was, he told me, *the proudest day* of his life.

Larry accomplished his financial goals in just under a year, which for the time was extraordinary. My father's achievement reflects his hard work, sacrifice and an overwhelming desire to get to a world where he would have a sense of home and community again. After his *baptism by fire,* my father was on his way to join his older siblings in America. He was thrilled to get out of Manchester and the smelly rooming house that had never felt like home. He posted a letter to his mother telling her he was going to America and would need time to get settled before he could send money again.

Larry was overwhelmed with excitement when he was able to purchase his one-way ticket to America aboard Trans World Airlines or what was popularly known by its abbreviated name as TWA. My dad possessed a new-found confidence as he boarded the plane for America, dressed in his new suit. Larry enthusiastically recounted the trip, explaining how he relished the airline meal, which was served on what my dad regarded as the finest china he had ever seen. He thought the flight attendants, or stewardesses as they were called in the 1950s, sensed it was his first flight, and were very kind and helpful. He recalls feeling quite *proper* on his journey to his new home in Boston. While other passengers slept, my father was too excited to sleep, but remembered the extended seats were the most comfortable he had ever enjoyed.

Larry's excitement was matched by his confidence as he now understood that his physical strength and willingness to work hard translated both on the farm and in the city. He never doubted his ability to *make it* in America since he had already done so under the most challenging conditions in Manchester. In America, Larry would have family and a sense of belonging again. For so many immigrants, like my dad, America was the land of opportunity, and Larry was determined to make the most of any chance he might get.

CHAPTER TEN:
A NEW NAME IN THE LAND OF OPPORTUNITY

My father was nearly 22 years old when he arrived at Boston's Logan International Airport on February 19, 1954. The first face he recognized was his older brother Mike who came to pick him up and remarked, *Jesus Larry, look at you.* My dad beamed as he interpreted his brother's comment as, *I'd never thought I'd see the day.* Mike directed Larry to his car, and my dad was quite impressed that his brother owned an auto of his own. *Jesus,* my dad thought, *'tis a great country.* Larry rode with Mike through the streets of Boston and on to their sister Mary's home in Dorchester, a six square-mile city neighborhood.

Dorchester was a popular destination for the Irish when my father arrived in America in the early 1950s. While small in square miles, Dorchester was thickly settled with just over 160,000 residents. Fully 93% of the population was white, and of the adult residents, 50% did not possess the equivalent of a high school diploma.[79] It was very much a working-class, affordable community and the Irish embraced it. The Irish population dominated Dorchester's social landscape so much so that the community was organized by parish. Instead of asking your street address, you were more likely to be asked, *what parish are you in?* Not until 1965 with the passage of the Nationality and Immigration Act would the complexity of Dorchester start to change.[80]

But during the 1950s it was a largely Irish immigrant community, and my father's siblings were among them. His sister Mary's home was the *Ellis Island,* of the now Cummings family. Married with children of her own, with the exception of Mike who was the first to emigrate, Mary housed all of her siblings upon their arrival in America until they could get established. Like his older siblings, Larry spent his first months in America with his sister's family.

After riding from the airport with Mike, my dad was welcomed to his new home by Mary and her husband Ben. Mary showed my dad to his bedroom and handed him towels, sheets and toiletries that included the first toothbrush Larry had ever owned. My dad was overwhelmed with his tidy room, which included a full-sized bed, chair, lamp and closet. He unpacked the few clothes he had in his suitcase and came downstairs to see his brother John and sister Peggy had arrived.

It was a joyous celebration as the siblings hugged and shared their stories of life developments since leaving Ireland. Mike was working at what my father described as a *desk job,* and had been taking evening courses to earn the equivalent of a high-school

---

79 Lima, Alvaro (Director). "Historical Trends in Boston Neighborhoods since 1950." *BPDA Research Division*, December 2017.
80 Johnson, Marilyn (Director). A Portal to the Regions Immigrants Past and Present. *Global Boston*, 2023.

diploma; Mary was married and she and her husband, who worked for the gas company, owned a home and had two children; John was apprenticing to be a carpenter; and Peggy, who had given thought to entering the convent, decided against it after spending three months cloistered with the Sisters of Saint Joseph, and she was working as a housekeeper. So much had happened in the seven years since Mike first departed Bornacurra followed quickly by Mary, John and Peggy. Larry told his siblings about his time in Manchester, and he felt quite proud that each commented on how quickly he had managed to save the money he needed to join them. They chatted for hours over a welcome dinner of ham, potatoes and beans, and my dad was thrilled to be eating so well. After dinner they had tea and Irish bread, and Larry turned the conversation to employment opportunities. My father was anxious to get to work, and it didn't take him long.

Sure, there were plenty of jobs back then. (Larry Cummings)

After more than a year in Manchester, Larry had found confidence in his ability to find work and make it on his own. While he was happy to be among family again, he did not arrive in Boston with the same fears that he felt in Manchester. My father found a job in Dorchester at a local baker's factory on his second day in America. He walked into the factory and asked for *the boss*, filled out an application and went to work. Larry's first job was short-lived, however, as he was fired when he pulled the wrong cord, dumping hundreds of pounds of flour on the floor (and covering a few co-workers in the process). But he was not defeated, and my father picked up a copy of the Boston Globe, which was delivered to his sister's home each day.

The Boston Globe, the most popular newspaper in the city when my father arrived, carried a section dedicated to employment advertisements.[81] It was there that Larry found an advertisement for a janitor at Harvard Medical School. With his sister's help, he found his way to Cambridge on the *T*, the popular term for the Massachusetts Bay Transportation Authority. His application led to a position as a janitor at Harvard Medical School's student dormitory.

Larry was excited to go to work as a janitor at the prestigious medical school. My dad got up at 5:00 a.m. and left his sister's home 30 minutes later, walking to the local train stop which took him to Cambridge. While his shift was 40 hours per week, Larry eagerly accepted any offer of overtime. As in Manchester, my dad's goal was to save as much money as possible.

Each day, medical students would arrive at the cafeteria for breakfast in the morning and dinner in the evening. While the students were at classes during the day preparing for their careers as future physicians, Larry was clearing the dishes, emptying the trash, washing the floors and scrubbing the bathrooms. When he was done cleaning the students' dining area and resident halls, he headed back to the kitchen to see if Chef needed anything else done.

Chef, as the staff called him, was the chief cook for the medical school cafeteria and my dad has many fond memories of him. A Black man in his thirties, Chef lived with his family in Boston's South End. The Black community in Boston, although less than 8% of the city's population when my father arrived, was growing throughout the 1950s. The Black community tended to live in Boston's South End and Roxbury sections. Like my dad, Chef took public transportation to work, and he may have ridden the train

---

81   See: https://globe.library.northeastern.edu/history-of-the-boston-globe/

with another South End resident, Martin Luther King, who was completing his Ph.D. at Boston University at that time.[82]

At the end of Larry's shift, Chef would always have a plate for him, and my dad looked forward to every meal since *Chef had a way with cookin'*. Larry recalled one Friday evening when the kitchen staff and my father enjoyed a special celebration. While my father couldn't remember the exact holiday, the medical students had left for a long weekend after Friday classes. Chef had not considered the holiday when ordering his food for the week and, as a result, he had an unintended surplus. Rather than waste it, Chef invited the kitchen staff and my dad to a special Friday evening steak dinner.

Chef, his assistant, the dishwasher, and Larry the janitor sat at the dining tables normally reserved for the medical students. Chef came out with steak, baked potato and corn for the main course, and followed it up with chocolate cake for dessert. Larry had never had steak before that day, and he remembers it as the most tasteful meal he had ever experienced. Chef told them he had more for them to take home after dinner and Larry knew his sister would be thrilled. While Mary had cooked wonderful meals that included protein in the form of chicken or ham, steak was a luxury that her budget couldn't accommodate.

Larry relished his first steak dinner and from that time on, whenever there was a family celebration, my dad insisted that steak was on the menu. Often, he would finish a steak dinner and comment how grand the meal was and ask, *Did I ever tell ya where I had my first steak dinner?* We, of course, knew the

---

[82] Today, a plaque is on the exterior wall of King's South End apartment at 397 Massachusetts Ave commemorating the time he lived there.

answer, it was in Harvard Medical School's dining hall, and Chef had prepared it.

The medical students could be a bit uppity ya know. One of them shouted for the cook and raised his voice, complainin' the meat wasn't cooked right. Chef came out and the student was rude and treated him badly, but Chef took it and said, "Sorry Sir," and went back into the kitchen and put it on the pan. Then he heated up the gravy, spat in it, and poured it all over the meat before delivering back to the student. We all had a good laugh watchin' him eat it. (Larry Cummings)

The year my father came to Harvard Medical School it was a bastion of white, male dominance. While women had been admitted nine years earlier and a handful of Black men had graduated since the school's inception in 1782, overwhelmingly, Harvard Medical School graduated white men.[83] From what my father regarded as *Yankee families,* America's future physicians were *rich people,* and had nothing in common with him or the cook he respected.

I asked my father about his interaction with medical students, and he was perplexed by the very question. *What do you mean? Sure, they never said a word to me. They just looked through ya, 'twas like I wasn't there.* Larry was invisible to the medical students whose bathrooms he cleaned, dishes he cleared, trash he emptied and floors he mopped. Not one student ever engaged Larry with a hello, good morning, or thank you in the time he worked as a janitor.

When Chef was rudely challenged by a medical student who was unhappy with his meal, he publicly responded with deference

---

83 See online at: https://hms.harvard.edu/about-hms/history-hms.

and called him, *sir*. But in his kitchen, Chef spat in the gravy that he poured over the student's meal, and in the process, sent a message that his staff, including my dad, understood and quietly cheered. On an ordinary day in 1954 in the dormitory kitchen at Harvard Medical School three Black, American-born men and one white Irish immigrant man laughed as a condescending white male and future physician *got his,* as Larry would say. It would be another decade before Chef's fellow South End resident, Martin Luther King, would give voice to the hope of the American dream for all. But in that moment, Chef and his staff, including my father, had a silent moment of triumph.

For my father, life was bifurcated between the rich and the poor, the haves and the have-nots. With what I would argue was a Marxian view of the economic world, Larry saw the *working man* and the *privileged rich*. He did not see skin color as a factor in economic struggles, because the construct of inferiority on the basis of skin color was foreign to him. The English had long been racist toward the Irish, not for their skin color, but for their belief that the Irish were an inferior race of people in the same way Hitler's Germany regarded the Jewish people as inferior.

For my dad, Chef was to be admired for a skill he did not have, his ability to cook excellent meals in large quantities. But Larry appreciated that he and Chef had far more in common than the students they served. Both men were thought to be inferior by the ruling class; both men worked hard for an hourly wage, and both never had the opportunities afforded Harvard's future physicians, nor would they ever enjoy their lifestyles or financial security. While Larry would say he didn't begrudge their success, he did feel the sting when one of his own, like Chef, had to absorb an insult from an *uppity* student.

Larry understood that Chef could never have challenged the student or called him out for an offensive tone or inappropriate language. In the same way, Larry accepted that he was an invisible man amid the affluent, educated Harvard Medical School elite. But he was grateful to have any job, and never complained. In fact, he was soon moved on to another job at Harvard.

Never be ashamed to take any job. If they ask ya to clean a toilet, make sure your toilets are the cleanest of the lot. And then they will notice ya, and say look what a good job he does, maybe he can do somethin' more. (Larry Cummings)

My father wholeheartedly believed in the *make sure your toilets are the cleanest* philosophy. While at Harvard Medical School Larry wasn't praised or thanked by the students, but he was noticed by the administration. Before my father arrived there had been frequent complaints about the lack of cleanliness in the dormitory bathrooms. But my dad took his philosophy to heart and would tell me when he was done cleaning a bathroom, *ya could eat off the floors.* That complaints ceased after his arrival was cause for notice and he was asked to come to the administration building. Larry was asked to expand his primary role to include faculty areas and to train new janitors who would take over his role in the medical school dormitories. Most importantly for Larry, he was given a significant pay raise.

What would become a near life-long career at Harvard University was launched after that meeting. Just as Larry had felt pride in being selected out of a group of working lads at Wimpey's in Manchester, he was now recognized at Harvard, again, for his hard work. His toilets were the cleanest, and he was moving on and up. As he left the full-time position in the medical school dormitory, Chef told my dad, *there is always a meal for you in my kitchen.*

Larry would take Chef up on his offer on more than one occasion. It wasn't long before his younger brother Tom was similarly emigrating to America and, like his older siblings, would be housed at Mary's Dorchester home. By the time Tom arrived, my dad had established himself and found a decent rooming house in Dorchester. Larry's new room was in an old Victorian home owned by an elderly woman, and he said, unlike Manchester, the room was very nice. The elderly owner offered to cook meals for her boarders for an extra charge, but Larry declined. He knew he could save a *bit of money* by dropping in at the Medical School cafeteria where Chef always took care of him.

Larry would remain at Harvard more than 40 years, moving from janitorial work to a skilled position as an operating engineer, taking care of heating and cooling systems. Regardless of the position he held, Larry always approached it the same way; show up on time, work hard and make sure your *toilets are the cleanest.* By the time he left Harvard, Larry was proud to say he had been promoted to boss.

But before arriving at the milestone as a manager, Larry had many years of work ahead. While his job at Harvard was Monday through Friday, my dad looked to make additional money on the weekend. Larry quickly realized that his farm skills could translate into seasonal landscaping work, and he had no trouble finding part-time opportunities.

In particular, there was high demand for landscaping services in affluent communities, like Brookline and Newton, which stood on the outskirts of the city of Boston. Both Brookline and Newton emerged as commuter communities longer before the suburban phenomenon that followed World War II.[84] Both communities had grand, single-family homes that frequently employed professional landscaping services.[85]

Larry easily found work in a full-service landscaping company that both maintained and customized lawns and gardens. Under the tutelage of talented landscape architects, Larry acquired a range of skills that served him well when he would later start his own side-business as a landscaper. My dad came to appreciate that quality landscaping was the result of more than hard work, but also required a knowledge base about which plants and shrubs should be planted in local climates and specifically how they should be cultivated for optimal growth. Lawn maintenance, Larry learned, was planned and included a number of processes like seeding, feeding and aerating. My father was now combining his work ethic with the essential knowledge and skill sets that produced optimal results.

Like so many Irish immigrants, Larry was acquiring the skills necessary to move from a life of subsistence to a life as part of America's middle-class.[86] It was a well-trodden path for the Irish since they had first emigrated to America in significant numbers following the Great Hunger. Like the Irish before him, my father's path toward fulfillment of the American dream and middle-class status would involve more than an economic journey. In the process, Larry would come to absorb the tragic legacy of America's *peculiar institution*.

---

84   Karr, Ronald Dale. *Between City and Country: Brookline Massachusetts, and the Origins of Suburbia*. University of Massachusetts Press, 2018.
85   For a history of efforts to prioritize single-family dwellings in Newton see: https://www.newtonma.gov/home/showpublisheddocument/67274/637517536459430000.
86   Historically, the term "middle class" has not been consistently used. In this context, I am using the term "middle class" to refer to an income that can support a family, provide health care and a measure of savings.

CHAPTER ELEVEN:
HOW THE IRISH BECAME WHITE

The Irish had faded from green to white, bleached by...something in the "atmosphere" of America. (Noel Ignatiev)[87]

In 1995 Harvard University graduate student and Marxist historian, Noel Ignatiev published his doctoral dissertation, *How the Irish Became White*, which burst out of the academic-publishing bubble into the mainstream discourse around issues of race and class in America. Ignatiev set out to understand in the years around the Civil War how the Irish had evolved from an oppressed, unwelcome social class to become part of the white, dominant class in America.

Going back to pre-revolutionary times, Ignatiev identified a parallel between the conditions of Irish-Catholics under British rule and American slaves. The English government regulated every aspect of Irish-Catholic lives through the Irish Penal Codes, which were first enacted in the 18th century. Among the myriad restrictions, the Penal Codes prohibited Irish-Catholics from voting, holding a military or civil service position, manufacturing

---

87   Ignatiev, Noel. *How the Irish Became White*. Routledge Press, 1995. Page 38.

or selling books, teaching in schools, or possessing a firearm. Moreover, Catholics could not receive an inheritance from Protestants, and male or female, Protestants who married Catholics lost their inheritance rights. Ignatiev drew a line between the oppressed Irish and American slaves citing the infamous dictum in the 1857 Dred Scot case where Supreme Court Chief Justice Roger Taney wrote, *The Negro has no rights a white man is bound to respect.*[88]

Like American slaves, Ignatiev argued, the Irish essentially had no rights that the British were bound to respect. Ireland had never known slavery within its borders and when the Irish emigrated to America they often lived among and worked with free Black Americans. Ignatiev claims that Irish ascendency into the oppressive white class was a conscious choice, a deliberate decision to abandon being green in favor of America's particular shade of white.

But I would argue that Ignatiev's assertion oversimplifies a complex and uneven process. First, Irish Americans always clung to their *green* identity, consistently voting as a block, and always in support of Irish causes. Irish Americans tenaciously clung to their Catholicism within a white, Protestant dominant culture. Some Irish, however, did see an end to slavery as a potential threat to their ability to secure unskilled jobs in the already low-paying labor market.

In 1863 in New York, for example, working-class Irish were the dominant force in what became known as the New York City

---

[88] Ibid. pp. 40-41. (Dred Scott had been born a slave but had been relocated to a free state and sued for his freedom on the grounds his time in a free state made him a free man. The case made its way to the Supreme Court which denied his claim and Taney's infamous dictum enraged abolitionists fueling the onset of the Civil War. For a summary, see: https://www.history.com/topics/black-history/dred-scott-case).

Draft Riots. Following President Lincoln's announcement of the Emancipation Proclamation, many Irish in New York feared the potential competition from newly freed slaves. Fear and insecurity were fueled with anger when the government announced that draftees who paid $300 could essentially "buy" a replacement in the war. In July 1863 Irish emotions overflowed into the streets where rioters attacked Protestant missions, Republican draft officials, wealthy businessmen, and freed Black workers. President Lincoln diverted troops from the Battle of Gettysburg to end the violence and restore order in the city. But the burden of the riots fell most heavily on Black workers, leaving hundreds dead, more than 3000 homeless and permanently altering the complexion of the city.[89]

In Boston, however, the Irish story during the Civil War was far different. Recent Irish immigrants to Boston were among the nearly 200,000 Irish who served the Union during the Civil War. Many made up what would become the All-Irish Brigade which garnered a celebrated reputation for its fierce and brave fighters.[90] In recognition, in 1863, the Commonwealth of Massachusetts approved the charter for Boston College, a Jesuit educational institution of higher education, which served an exclusively Irish-Catholic populace in its early years.[91]

What these two very different Irish experiences demonstrate is that while the Irish were in some ways a monolithic force in American history, they, like all immigrants, were shaped by forces

---

89 There are a number of excellent books on the draft riots, see particularly, Bernstein, Iver. *The New York City Draft Riots: Their Significance for American Society and Politics in the Age of the Civil War.* Oxford University Press, 1991.
90 O'Brien, Kevin E. and Bilby, Joseph G. *The History of the Irish Brigade: A Collection of Historical Essays.* Sergeant Kirkland's Press, 1997.
91 https://www.bc.edu/content/dam/files/publications/factbook/pdf/98_99/fb99mission-history.pdf

specific to their day-to-day lives. Ignatiev's argument that the Irish *chose* to become white in order to solidify their economic place in American society is an overreaching position. I would argue, however, that what is most compelling about his work is not in its bold assertions, but the subtle and timeless implications of his argument.

In *How the Irish Became White*, Ignatiev quotes a Boston Irishman who says, *Colored people did not know their place*. The author goes on to ask, *How, I wondered, did an Irish immigrant, perhaps fresh off the boat, learn "the place" of a negro*?[92] Herein lies the most valuable question in Ignatiev's work.

The Irish in America, including my father and his siblings, would come to accept racist assumptions as they moved into their white, middle-class, suburban worlds. But it was less a conscious choice than a slow, often imperceptible, absorption of the dominant values around them. It took time and was not present when they arrived in the promised land. America's brand of racism was nonexistent in Ireland, and when my father arrived in Boston he aligned with his boss, Chef and his fellow black coworkers. They were the *working men* who saw themselves in opposition to the affluent white medical students they served. In the same way, his brother John was shocked to encounter the racism that existed in America's south.

Following their wedding in the 1956, John and his new bride Kay decided to take a honeymoon journey through the east coast of the United States. My uncle had purchased a new car and was excited to explore his new homeland with his bride. The couple set out from Boston, drove on to New York and down into the south.

---

92   Ignatiev, p. 207.

Their plan was to go as far as Florida and then return home. John and Kay stopped at a *filling station* in South Carolina, which had a small grocery store attached. And there, my uncle and his wife received a lesson in race relations from a local police officer.

John and Kay got gas and then went into the store to pick up a few items to take on their journey. Together, they were in line behind a Black woman and her young child as she attempted to buy milk and bread. The store clerk told the woman, *we don't serve niggers here,* and the mother walked away with her child, leaving her milk and bread on the counter. My uncle was in shock that anyone would refuse to sell staples to a mother with a child in tow. He stepped up to the counter, bought his items and the milk and bread left behind by the Black woman. He followed the woman outside the store and called out, *Ma'am, here, take your milk and bread.* The woman tried to pay my uncle, but he refused telling her it was his pleasure. Clearly discerning his brogue, the mother asked John where he was from, and my uncle told her Ireland. She smiled, thanked him and John smiled telling her, *you're welcome—you have a fine boy Ma'am.*

John and Kay got in their car and proceeded on their journey for about a mile when a police cruiser came up behind them with sirens blaring. My uncle wasn't speeding and said he had no idea what he had done wrong. John pulled over and was asked to step outside his vehicle. The policeman asked my uncle where he was from and when he told him Ireland, the officer told him he needed to learn how things were done *down here.* Using his baton, he punched my uncle in the stomach and walked away, leaving him on the ground on the side of the road. John and Kay ended their honeymoon trip on the spot and set out to return to Boston wondering, *what kind of country have we moved to?*

Both Larry and John, along with their other siblings, came face-to-face with a brand of racism that was foreign to them. While they intimately understood discrimination on the basis of nationality and religious preference, racism on the basis of skin color was new to them, and it was specific to their new, celebrated homeland. While Ignatiev saw it as a choice, I would argue it was an absorption, far more subtle but no less detrimental. Sadly, white, Irish immigrants did absorb many of the racist assumptions that were widely held when they arrived in America in the 1950s. And their first teachers were among the generation who had emigrated before them.

When my father and his siblings arrived in America they were all welcomed by the generation that had come before them on both their father and mother's sides of the family. Both Paddy and Nora had extensive families in America, all of whom lived in the Greater Boston area. It was one of Paddy's brothers who sponsored my Uncle Mike when he emigrated as the first in their generation to leave Ireland for America.

The initial goal was always the same for Irish arrivals—secure a job. And Larry and his siblings were among many Boston Irish immigrants who easily found work. While the overwhelming majority performed entry-level manual labor jobs, for the Irish who had been in Boston for multiple generations, many had moved up the social ladder. As O'Connor points out in his political history of the Boston Irish:

On a more modest level, the upward mobility of Irish-Catholic families during the early part of the twentieth century allowed them to save a little money and send a son to college (usually the first in the family's history), and eventually move out of the old two-decker to a single family in Milton or West Roxbury, where they became part of the so-called lace-curtain Irish. Bright young men and women from Irish American families competed for openings as teachers, policemen, firemen, nurses, custodians, librarians, and clerks, while others found equally desirable jobs in the telephone company, the gas company, and the electric company, or as streetcar conductors, motormen for the Boston elevated Railway, or salesmen in downtown insurance companies.[93]

What O'Connor did not address in his political history of the Irish in Boston is the racism many absorbed as they climbed the social ladder. Contrary to Ignatiev, I argue the process of *becoming white* is gradual, often imperceptible. It is the racist joke my father listened to as a young man and found himself telling suburban friends in middle-age. Learning America's racist assumptions in the 1950s was like developing cancer; it was insidious in that for the longest time you could not detect it until one day it was a full-grown tumor.

My father's uncles and aunts were among the lace curtain Irish when he arrived in America in 1954. All of them were enjoying life in Boston's white suburban neighborhoods, and they were who Larry and his siblings wanted to be someday. As the next generation of immigrants attended family gatherings at what my dad would later describe as *fancy barbeques*, they observed and sought to emulate the lifestyles of those who had *made it*.

The Irish in 1950s America were in the midst of a post-war boom, which enjoyed an economy marked by both low unemployment and inflation. As a result of the G.I. Bill, millions of WWII Veterans had access to higher education and, as a

---

[93] Thomas H. O'Connor, *The Boston Irish: A Political History*, Northeastern University Press, 1995, page 223.

consequence, upward mobility. All of America was in the midst of an expansion of the interstate highway system, which was traversed by a now common purchase, the family car. Wages were rising and American purchasing power was steadily increasing.[94]

For Larry and his siblings, it was a good time to be in America, and *making it* was an attainable goal. After all, they had been eating hamburgers and hot dogs at the homes of relatives who had already done so. With their role models in place, my dad and his siblings had confidence that their futures were optimistic. But they also came to appreciate that *making it* was far easier for white citizens, and white supremacy was justified on the foundation of racist assumptions that could be traced to the era of American slavery.

The year Larry arrived in Boston U.S. Supreme Court Justice Earl Warren delivered the unanimous ruling in the landmark civil rights case *Brown v. Board of Education of Topeka, Kansas*, which ruled state-sanctioned segregation of public schools was a violation of the 14th amendment and, therefore, unconstitutional.[95] The following year, Rosa Parks, a Black activist, was arrested in Montgomery, Alabama for refusing to give up her seat on a city bus to white man, launching a boycott of some 17,000 Black citizens.[96] But the early years of the Civil Rights Movement seemed distant and irrelevant to Larry and his siblings. They focused on their immediate goals, getting established and moving on and up to the suburbs.

Within five years of his arrival Larry would follow his brothers and sisters to the suburbs of Boston where all the men would find

---

94 There are a plethora of books on the 1950s but David Halberstam's, *The Fifties* is comprehensive and still holds up today. Ballantine Books, 1993.
95 https://www.archives.gov/milestone-documents/brown-v-board-of-education#:~:text=On%20May%2017%2C%201954%2C%20U.S.,amendment%20and%20was%20therefore%20unconstitutional.
96 There are a number of books and documentaries on Rosa Parks. With Jim Haskins, she published *Rosa Parks: My Story*. Scholastics Inc., 1992.

work that could sustain a living wage. With union protection, benefits, and the ability to work over-time, newly arrived Irish, like my father, could own a modest home, put food on the table and provide health care for their families. There was also the possibility that their children could go to college and achieve even more success. The economic path that was available to Irish immigrants, like my parents, facilitated their association with white America and their absorption of the racist assumptions that accompanied it. America was truly the promised land for my father's family and countless other Irish. And if they wanted to dream big, all they had to do was look to the Kennedy family as model of what was possible in America.

Two years before my father's arrival John Kennedy had won a seat in the U.S. Senate, defeating Henry Cabot Lodge, Jr., a *scion of Boston Brahmin's class who traced his ancestors back to the Puritans.*[97] The rise of the Kennedy family was a point of pride among all Irish Catholics. At once, the family's success validated the Irish as worthwhile Americans, offered hope to future generations, and gave Boston Irish in the mid-century a candidate they could stand behind. For my father, it was a good time to be in America. And it was important to my dad to be fully American.

The law allowed immigrants to apply for citizenship after five years of residency in the country. My father would waste no time submitting his application in 1959. At that time, he could also change his name to Cummings, and follow suit with all male members of his family. Larry recounted studying for his exam to become an American citizen and was enthralled with the history of his new homeland. He came to love history and I believe,

---

[97] See Michael Quinlan, *Irish Boston: A Lively look at Boston's Colorful Irish Past*, Globe Pequot Press, 2013.pp. 130-131.

conveyed his passion to me. Throughout his life Larry wore a pin on his suit lapel that displayed the combined flags of Ireland and the Unites States of America. He was a proud Irish American who took his children to Washington D.C. where we toured the White House and several museums. But before Larry arrived at citizenship and family life, he needed to find a wife.

I definitely wanted an Irish girl—you always want to stay with your own people. (Larry Cummings)

There would be no question in my father's mind that his future wife would be Irish. He told me he couldn't have imagined marrying anyone that wasn't part of *his own people.* There was a comfort level, Larry explained, in marrying someone who understood things in the ways you did. And, of course, children would be raised Catholic.

While Ignatiev had argued that on their journey to *whiteness* the Irish abandoned their *greenness*, I would posit that they tenaciously maintained the Irish component of Irish American, while at the same time learning to become white in America. Racist assumptions, widely held in the 1950s, were part of the learned Irish experience when they arrived in their new homeland. And for Irish immigrants, like my father, it is unlikely it would have been any different.

Foremost, the Irish were socialized to be humble, and not to challenge authority. It takes thoughtful reflection, confidence and boldness to stand up to the status quo. My father did not possess those qualities in the 1950s, and I would suggest few Irish immigrants did. They focused on making a living and took their social cues from those who had immigrated before them. Family barbeques had been instructive, and the subtle racist cues that pervaded the 1950s were slowly absorbed. But for my father, the suburban dream was still a distant reality.

Larry had begun to establish himself economically, and the next step in his journey toward suburban success was to establish a family. Like many of the Irish in the 1940s and 1950s, he met his future spouse at the Irish dances that were so popular when my father arrived in Boston.[98] On Dudley Street, at the Intercolonial Hall in Roxbury, Larry met his future bride, an Irish girl from Kerry. From a romantic dance in a Boston dance hall in 1956, their story returns to Ireland, and to the hills of Kerry.

---

98   For a thorough look at the Irish music and dance scene, see Susan Gedutis, *See You at the Hall: Boston's Golden Era of Irish Music and Dance*. Northeastern University Press, 2004.

CHAPTER TWELVE:
ELIZABETH, THE KERRY GIRL

Everything about her was different. Elizabeth Carey was an only child at a time Irish couples had large broods of children. She was doted on by an older, loving mother at a time and place where most rural Irish children just got through the day. Born November 19, 1934, Elizabeth Carey was the daughter of two distantly related cousins, Daniel Carey and Katherine Carey. They married in their thirties, and my mother came into their lives ten years later.

Me and you could be wed yet. Dan Carey's proposal to Kate. (Recounted by Betty Cummings)

Like my grandfather and grandmother on my father's side, my maternal grandmother, Katherine, or Kate as she was called, might have had a very different life. She was born in County Kerry but had left for America as a young woman, arriving in Boston in 1915, just months after Nora. It is certainly possible that she may have been among the Irish-immigrant domestics who gathered to celebrate Nora's engagement and farewell celebration as she headed back to Bornacurra to marry her fiancé, Paddy.

Unlike Nora and the great majority of Irish domestics, Kate was a skilled cook and superlative baker. Within a year of her arrival, Kate moved to Newburyport, a coastal city 35 miles north of Boston. Her reasons for doing so appear to be work-related.

Kate's Boston-based position did not give her the opportunity to develop her talents, and when a more appealing position was posted in the Boston newspaper, Kate applied. She traveled to her interview aboard the Boston and Maine Railroad, which at that time, had a stop in Newburyport.[99] After a short trial, Kate was hired full time, as the chief cook and baker, a position she would remain in for over ten years.

Newburyport was considerably smaller than Boston with a population of just over 15,000 when Kate arrived.[100] Compared to Boston's 750,000 this was quite a change for Kate. She may have enjoyed the coastal community's quieter pace, and she certainly enjoyed her work and seems to have respected her employers. But Kate struggled to meet young, available Irish men. On occasion, Kate did travel by train to Boston to meet up with friends and socialize, but she never developed a sustained relationship with a potential marriage partner. Like so many Irish in America, it was important to Kate to marry one of *her own people.*

As her 30th birthday approached, Kate was at a crossroads and through letters home to her parents they suggested that she return home to Ireland. They informed Kate that a distant cousin, Dan, was going to inherit his family farm, and he would be an excellent marriage partner. Discussions between the two families

---

[99] The Boston & Maine Railroad was at its peak in the early 1920s. With the expansion of automobile sales and travel, the railroad began to decline. See Heald, Bruce. *A History of the Boston & Maine Railroad*, Arcadia Press, 2007.

[100] "Census - Geography Profile: Newburyport city, Massachusetts". United States Census Bureau. Retrieved March 2023.

ensued and it was agreed that Kate would surrender part of her savings as a dowry for Dan's sister but maintain a more significant amount as her own dowry.

Kate heeded her parents' advice, bought a one-way ticket on a ship that departed from New York and arrived in Ireland some three weeks later. Her parents promptly introduced her to Dan and Kate found him to be kind. His sister promptly married a neighboring villager who was similarly destined to inherit his family's farm, and his brother booked a passage to America. Given that Kate had worked for more than a decade as a cook and baker, she would have earned more than most Irish domestics, and it is likely that her future brother-in-law's passage to America was booked using her dowry.

The Carey's small farm was in a rural village, just outside the town of Killorglin in County Kerry. Today the area is a popular tourist destination; and, as part of the *Ring of Kerry,* is known for its natural beauty, access to both ocean front and lakes, and tranquil charm. But the idea of tourism would be many years off, and when Dan's family inhabited the area, they were just one of many village farmers. The Careys' modest holding provided sustenance levels of dairy, vegetables, and the occasional bacon and beef supplied by a few pigs and cows. Like all homes in rural Ireland at the time, there was no indoor plumbing, nor was there a specific outhouse. It wasn't glamorous, but Dan was now a man with a place, and Kate was happy to be home among family again. She accepted his very practical proposal of marriage, and Kate never returned to America again.

Kate moved into the Carey family cottage following her modest church wedding to Dan. The home that housed the newly married couple and her in-laws featured an open room with a central fireplace, and two small bedrooms off to each side. In his parents' time, the Carey cottage had the standard, thatched roof. But by the time Dan and Kate married, the roof had been converted to slate, and the dirt floors were covered in cement. In the rear of the cottage was a cold room, a small, partially below-grade room with a slanted roof, designed to hold bacon and beef after a cow or pig was slaughtered. Dan and Kate lived with Dan's parents in the cottage for over ten years before their only child arrived.

My mother, Betty has no memory of her grandmother, who died when she was quite young. But she does remember a loving grandfather, Dennis, who slept in the smaller, second bedroom. Betty shared a bedroom with her parents, they in a full-sized bed, and she at the opposite side of the room in a single bed. Not unlike my father's home, sleeping arrangements had more to do with practicality than privacy. But the family of four were happy, as my mother often said, *it was a good life.*

We couldn't brag, but we had what the other guy had. (Betty Cummings)

The Careys were not well-off, but as my mother recalls they had what their neighbors similarly enjoyed, a roof over their heads, food on the table, and warm clothes to wear in the cold months. But more than her neighbors, my mother recalls a life of advantages that were not afforded her village friends who came from large families. As an only child with older parents well into their forties, my mother recalls being doted on.

My mother was awfully upset when I kept coming home with head lice, so she went to the school master to complain. He passed out the DDT and the problem went away. (Betty Cummings).

Every evening Kate sat by the fire and combed Betty's long, blond hair. Head lice were not uncommon during my parents' childhood, and my grandmother carefully removed the active lice and eggs from my mother's scalp, only to see them return again-and-again after she returned to school. Her mother was determined to put a stop to it and visited the school master insisting he act. The school responded by dispensing DDT (Dichlorodiphenyltrichloroethane), an insecticide, known to kill insects of all kinds, but later found to be a dangerous carcinogenic. But during the 1940s and 1950s it was commonly dispensed. Her classmates used the insecticide, and Kate got the result she wanted; her daughter's lice did not return. Interestingly, my grandmother did not use DDT on my mother. Rather, she took comfort in that the other children did, and preferred to remove head lice the old-fashioned way—picking out the eggs from her daughter's infected locks.

It is likely that if Kate had had a large brood of children she would not have had the time, nor inclination, to worry about something as minor as head lice. But as the sole object of Kate's time and affection, my mother experienced a far different upbringing than my father. She recalls a wardrobe that included a number of pretty dresses, some store-bought, and others hand-made by her mother, fancy shoes for Sunday Mass, and pennies from her grandfather to purchase candies in town. Since they were a small family, there was always plenty to eat, and protein in the form of bacon and beef was a weekly staple at the Carey household.

Typical for their time, the Careys split chores along gender lines. Dan tended to the pigs and cows and tilled the soil, while Kate looked after the chickens, cooked, cleaned, hand-washed clothing and looked after their only child. My mother was more a *helper* than a farm worker. Betty would collect eggs, hang laundry, and stir the flour mixture that produced Kate's exceptional breads, cakes and pies. Kate would occasionally take my mother to the local town where she would sell eggs and hand-churned butter, along with breads and rolls. Kate's baking was well-known and always sold out, which provided the family with extra cash for luxuries.

In addition, Kate's monetary contribution to the Carey household allowed them to purchase a few livestock, which were a source of both income and food. To contribute to the family's cash flow Dan also sold turf from time-to-time, and the occasional calf. But a portion of the Careys cash flow came from the expanding Irish welfare state.

We called it the dole, and it was very common in our area. (Betty Cummings)

Throughout the 1930s and 1940s Ireland expanded social welfare programs to include unemployment assistance, as well as pensions for widows, orphans and the elderly.[101] My mother recalls a number of her fellow villagers were *on the dole*. The Carey farm was modest by the day's standards and provided enough food for their small family. But had the Careys produced a larger brood, which would have been the norm, their farm could not have sustained them. In the hills of Kerry there was little work available, and Dan did not have outside employment, leaving him eligible for government assistance. In addition, my mother's grandfather would also have been eligible for a senior's pension, increasing the cash flow into the Carey household.

The combination of government assistance, a small farm, and a single child meant the Careys lived a relatively comfortable

---

[101] Adrian Kelly, "*Catholic Action and the Development of the Irish Welfare State in the 1930s and 1940s.*" Catholic Historical Society of Ireland, Vol. 53, pp. 107-117 (1999).

life. Although my father's family had a larger farm, and an income from their father's employment, with four adults and eight children to feed, they barely got by. Unlike my father, my mother enjoyed luxuries my father couldn't have imagined. In addition to store bought clothing, she recalls routine trips into town where she enjoyed the occasional American film and treats from the sweet shop.

My mother does not recall any negative stigma attached to the dole. That the government should assist its needy seems to have been accepted by its populace and supported by the Catholic Church.[102] And while my mother enjoyed a much higher standard of living than her peers, for large families, social welfare likely enabled sheer survival. But, in spite of the benefits my mother enjoyed as an only child, she recalls desperately wanting a sibling.

There is nothing to be done; babies are found under bushes. (Betty Cummings quoting her mother Kate)

As a young girl, my mother inquired why she didn't have a brother or sister. Babies were everywhere in the homes of her village friends, and it confused her why she was alone. Her mother explained that there was nothing that could be done; babies, she said, were found under bushes, and you either got one or you did not. My mother was naïve enough to accept her explanation and recalled looking through bushes for weeks trying to find a baby to bring home to the Carey farm.

Just a few years later, the Carey family was assisting a cow as it gave birth. My mother recalls how pained the cow looked as it pushed its baby into the world. *Can you imagine, Ma'am, if women had to do that?* she asked her mother. Her mother's

---

[102] See again Adrian Kelly.

response was short and direct: *They do, Betty.* And that was my mother's first introduction to sex education.

Not unlike my father's experience, my mother recalls that sex was never openly discussed in her rural world, even though it permeated the farming experience. My grandmother never brought the subject up again, and my mother, speechless at her mother's statement, would have to learn what she meant through observation, and later, peer interaction.

Dan, that is enough now. (Elizabeth Cummings quoting her mother Kate)

Betty was 5'5", with a slender frame, blue eyes and a thick head of long, blonde hair. Regarded as pretty, Kate became particularly concerned when her daughter started to menstruate at 14 years of age. My grandmother kept a watchful eye on my mother's monthly menses to ensure that *nothing happened to [her]*. Kate supervised the cleaning of Betty's menstrual rags each month, which she hung on a rack behind the house so a visitor wouldn't see them. Kate also ensured that if Betty were in the company of the opposite sex, she was carefully supervised.

It took a few years more before my mother fully understood the connection between menstruation, sex and pregnancy; and when she finally understood, she was able to backfill childhood experiences. For example, she now understood the noises she heard at night in her parents' bed, and her mother telling her father, *Dan that is enough now.* And she understood what a local village boy had been after when he came to her home when her parents were in town. He had tried to get close to her, and it made Betty feel very uncomfortable, so much so that she screamed at him to get out and threatened to tell her parents. The boy left immediately, without violating her, and Betty never reported the visit to her parents. Understanding sexuality, then, was a process of gut feelings, peer interaction, visual observation, parental cues, and for many like my mother, unfortunate encounters.

Sexual lessons were similarly communicated at mass where the Catholic teaching was definitive and strict. Both my parents concur that nothing was said overtly, but sitting in the pew each week, the lessons were clear. Blaygards and dillies were going straight to hell. My mother got a steady dose of fiery sermons as she attended weekly mass sitting beside her mother, while her father sat on the opposite side of church with the other village men and boys. But, while the Catholic Church in rural Ireland during the 1930s and 1940s pumped out a steady diatribe around behavioral codes, it had no issue with the annual pagan festival, the Puck Fair.[103]

Every August in Killorglin, Kerry the locals gather to celebrate the oldest known fair in Ireland, the Puck Fair. In Irish, the translation is *Aonach an Phoic*, or "Fair of the He-Goat." A goat is captured, placed in a cage and hoisted onto an elevated stage where it remains for three days until it is released into the mountains. The town's streets are flooded with vendors selling their wares, and pubs stay open well into the night. While there are a number of legends that surround the fair's origins, scholars generally believe it can be traced to pre-Christian Ireland as a harvest celebration. That the goat was a pagan symbol of fertility seems to confirm this.

Betty remembers the annual fair as one of the most exciting times of year, and her mother was frequently a vendor, selling her tasty, sweet treats. She also recalls that everyone attended,

---

[103] Langan, Sheila, Ed. "Puck Fair: Ireland's Oldest Festival." *Irish America*, October 2011.

including local parish priests. That Catholic priests would attend a pagan fair in Ireland during my mother's childhood is not surprising. Irish Catholicism, particularly in rural areas, seemed to meld together Catholic dogma with local values and traditions. No one would have questioned how this pagan tradition lived in parallel with Catholic beliefs. But while tolerant of pre-Christian traditions, there were areas where the Catholic Church in Ireland dominated. Among them, was the education of Irish youth. As in my father's case in Galway, my mother also confirmed that Catholic teachings were consistently reinforced in school.

I wasn't the brightest, but I was an excellent speller, and very good at sums. (Betty Cummings)

Unlike my father, my mother enjoyed school. She recalls being average in most subjects, but exceptional in both spelling and sums, basic arithmetic. And while my father never received the Irish equivalent of a high school diploma, or leaving certificate, my mother was awarded the distinction at the age of fourteen. Routinely my mother and her school friends *met down the road*, a gathering place for chat, games and adolescent bantering. Like my father, my mother recalls the gatherings were innocent enough, although occasionally, there would be the *odd cigarette* past around that had been lifted from a parent's case. Like Larry, my mother lived in an innocent time when parents did not have to worry about drugs, shootings, and the invasive nature of social media. Unlike my dad, however, Betty's memories of her childhood were consistently happy ones.

Betty was fortunate to have escaped corporal discipline at school, although she recalls a number of students being whipped for all sorts of transgressions from arriving late to talking or forgetting homework. My mother remembers feeling guilty and sad as she watched friends being strapped. *I would close my eyes and hope it ended quickly. I'd feel lucky it wasn't me, but then I would feel guilty all the same.*

Betty was also free from corporal discipline at home. Dan and Kate never physically punished their daughter, choosing to explain why they and God expected better behavior from her. My mother understood this was not the norm among her peers, and she felt lucky. As a child, Betty felt very much loved and wanted, even doted upon.

While my father's family was large and always on the edge of subsistence, my mother remembers being treated to special presents, especially at Christmas. Betty's favorite memory is getting a doll inside her Christmas stocking when she was about seven years old. Kate hand-made outfits for the doll so her daughter could play dress-up, and Betty would play and sleep with that doll throughout most of her childhood.

In addition to the occasional present, Kate frequently made sweet pies, cakes and rolls for her family. My mother remembers neighbors would frequently come for tea and rave about Kate's baking skills. While it was a happy childhood for my mother, the hills of Kerry offered little as young children transitioned into adulthood. By the time adolescents reached fifteen, the overwhelming majority were looking ahead to life beyond Ireland.

The last dance was rather sad because you knew you might not see them again. (Betty Cummings)

After graduation my mother was old enough to attend the social highlight of the village, the local dance. She paid four pence to get in, which covered the cost of the fiddler and a bowl of orange-flavored soft drink. There, village adolescents met up, danced and talked about their coming adventures. My mother recounted that at nearly every dance, there would be an announcement regarding an upcoming departure of a local villager to either England or America. He or she would receive the honor of closing the evening by dancing *the last dance* of the night. With the applause of friends and siblings, the evening ended as feelings of happiness, anticipation and, for some, sadness permeated the walk home.

I was 16 and it was time to leave. There was nothing for me at home. (Betty Cummings)

My mother remained home after graduation for nearly two years but left at age sixteen to begin work in service to an affluent city family. Betty's first job was in the city of Killarney, cooking and cleaning for a clothing store owner and his wife and three children. My mother has mixed recollections about her first work experience. While the store owner was pleasant, and the children fun, the lady of the house, a stay-at-home mother, was difficult and demanding. My mother had learned to cook from her mother, who had exceptional skills. But my mother's house had an open fireplace, and Betty had no experience with modern-day ovens. The transition must have produced less than stellar meals, which upset her boss. Cleaning came much easier, and with six days on and one day off, there was ample time to clean their nice, but modest urban home. For Irish, urban, middle-class families, hired help was plentiful and inexpensive as young rural girls flocked from the countryside to earn wages to help support their families and save money for their ultimate destinations, England and America.

My mother was no different than her village peers in her desire to leave Ireland for opportunities abroad. Kate discouraged her daughter from going to England, telling Betty that, *bad things happen there*. As a result, my mother set her eyes on Boston, a popular destination among her friends. She had exchanged letters with other village girls who lived and worked in Boston, and they all encouraged Betty to come. After working for two years, my mother had saved enough for a passage to Boston and was excited about her future abroad in America. Her first step was to secure her passport, and when Betty went to get her birth certificate, she was shocked to discover there was no record of an Elizabeth Carey from her village.

CHAPTER THIRTEEN:
"THE GIRL DOWN THE ROAD": ELIZABETH'S SHAMEFUL SECRET

Your name isn't Carey, it's Golden. (Betty Cummings quoting her boss)

My mother learned she was illegitimate the day she went into the city to get a copy of her birth certificate. Betty was told there was no record of any Elizabeth Carey in her village on file, and she left the county office confused and uncertain of what the problem might be. After all, all of her friends who had previously departed for England or America got their passports without an issue. Betty could not understand how there was no record of her birth on file. Betty returned to her place of employment and told her boss that the county office insisted there was no record of an Elizabeth Carey. Her boss' answer was direct and to the point, explaining that her name wasn't Carey, it was Golden. At that moment, my mother learned that Dan and Kate Carey were not her biological parents.

Kate had told Betty's employers about her illegitimate status prior to her arrival at their home. Her reason for doing so is not clear. Perhaps she worried that if they found out they might fire her daughter, and it was best to tell them in advance. Kate had also informed them that my mother was unaware of her illegitimate status, and she would like to keep it that way. Her employers honored their promise until my mother was confronted with the harsh reality that she could not be Elizabeth Carey, since no such person existed. A young Betty returned home to confront her parents feeling shocked, frightened and confused.

Hannah Golden is your mother. (Betty Cummings quoting her mother)

Hannah was the *girl down the road,* the daughter of the Goldens who were village neighbors. She was unwed and barely eighteen years old when she gave birth to my mother at home. Since Dan and Kate had never had children, they were approached by Hannah's parents and asked to take her newborn in. Kate was a warm woman with a kind heart, and she longed for a child. Her husband Dan also agreed that a baby girl would be a welcome addition to the Carey family. Kate and Dan eagerly brought their new baby girl into their home, named her Elizabeth, nicknamed her Betty, and always referred to her as a Carey. The adoption was not official, and had my mother decided to stay in Ireland, she might have lived and died in her village never knowing the truth.

Shortly after giving birth to my mother, Hannah moved to England where she married an Irish laborer, with the surname, O'Leary. To my mother's knowledge, she had a least one child, a son, Patrick, my mother's half-brother. My mother knew of her from neighbors who regularly shared news of their children abroad in England and the States. And while people in her village would certainly have known about the adoption, like most things connected to sexuality, especially illicit sexuality, it was never discussed. As the Irish were fond of saying, *the less said about it, the better.*

My mother felt a visceral anger toward her parents for keeping her in the dark about the reality of her lineage. Her father explained that he always wanted to tell her, but Kate insisted it remain a secret. As Betty cried and shouted, *how could you lie all this time*, a tearful Kate could only say, *I am sorry, I love you so much*.

In that moment, so many things suddenly made sense to Betty. Kate was in her forties when she and Dan adopted my mother, because they were incapable of having biological children. Now Betty understood why she was an only child and why she had enjoyed a childhood not experienced by any other children in her village. Kate was overjoyed to have a child of her own and tended to spoil her adopted daughter. Betty also understood why her mother had warned her against going to England, telling her, *bad things happen there*. Kate was fearful that Betty would encounter her biological mother.

When my mother and I discussed the revelation that she was illegitimate I certainly appreciated the shock and anger she felt. But I did ask her if she would have changed anything. *After all*, I said, *you had so much love, so many material comforts relative to your peers, and you never experienced physical punishment like dad did*. My mother's response was clear: *I would have taken a hundred beatings rather than hear the news I got that day*. Given Irish attitudes toward illegitimacy, my mother's response is not surprising.

From the formation of free Ireland in 1922 through 1952, all adoptions in the country were technically long-term foster placements and only semi-legal at best and completely illegal at worse. Ireland would not have an official Adoption Act until 1952. Passed under de Valera's government, the act legally branded babies born outside wedlock as "illegitimate" and essentially assigned them second-class legal status. For example, "illegitimate" people were banned from joining the Garda (Irish police force) by the state and banned by the church from becoming priests without special papal dispensation. Not until 1987 was the status revoked.[104]

That adoptions were not handled legally when my mother was born, explains why the Careys never pursued legal guardianship of their adopted daughter. Moreover, that the Irish government would legally define children born out of wedlock as second-class citizens nearly twenty years after my mother was born, suggests how such a status was viewed in 1934. My mother would become a grandmother before Ireland reversed the Adoption Act, removing the term illegitimate and restoring full legal status to all children, regardless of the marital status of their parents.

As a young woman, my mother was utterly broken by the devastating news of the circumstances around her birth. She told me it took her years to *get over it,* and I suspect she never truly did. At first, it was extraordinarily hard for Betty to even discuss it. While my mother had no control over the circumstances, she felt deeply ashamed to be the product of an illegitimate union. Betty told me she always felt *less than,* like she was *unworthy.*

Moreover, Betty also felt angry and abandoned by her biological mother. And since Betty knew where Hannah lived in England, she decided to write her a letter. For my mother, it was a therapeutic attack from a wounded, and deeply saddened 18-year-old whose world had been turned upside down in a single day. Betty could not have put herself in her biological mother's shoes, and imagined how ostracized she must have felt, how

---

[104] Abby, Sean Ross. *Report into the History of Adoption in the Irish Free State since 1922.* July 2013.

ashamed her family would have felt, and how the adoption, and her departure for England, was Hannah's only viable option.

Living as a single mother in Ireland in the 1930s would not have been tolerated, and her family would never have kept her baby. Moreover, after giving birth to my mother, Hannah would not have any chance of a marriage in Ireland. But my mother couldn't appreciate Hannah's dilemma; she could only feel her own pain, her sense of abandonment, and her anger for having lived for so long under a cloud of lies.

Betty wrote Hannah a scathing letter, telling her she was glad that Hannah had given her up, that she had a wonderful mother who was a far better person than Hannah would ever be. Betty concluded by telling Hannah she never wanted to hear from her. Kate Carey cried when she read the letter her daughter was sending to her biological mother, and the two of them walked together into town to post it.

There were lots of stories about it, I never knew for sure. (Betty Cummings)

My mother's birth certificate reflects that she was born on November 19, 1934, to Johanna Golden in her family home on Traler Road, Castlemaine, County Kerry. A midwife, Catherine Sullivan, was present at her birth. The section where the father's name would be recorded was blank, with a diagonal line through the box. I asked my mother about her father, but she had little information. She was told her mother had been in England working, became pregnant, returned home to have the baby, and then went back to England to resume working after her birth. But this story seems unlikely.

First, DNA testing confirms that my siblings and I are fully Irish, with our gene pool originating from our parents' homes in

Galway and Kerry. It is certainly possible that Hannah traveled to England and became pregnant by a boy from Kerry, but it is highly unlikely that an Irish village family in the early 1930s would welcome home their pregnant daughter, assist her in giving birth, and then arrange an unofficial adoption before sending her back to England.

It is far more likely that Hannah became pregnant while she was in Ireland, delivered my mother and then departed for England. That begs the question: Why wasn't Hannah's pregnancy legitimated by marriage? If her father were a local boy, why didn't he marry Hannah? It may be that the father left for England or America, or it may be that he lived locally but was unavailable to marry Hannah. But it is also possible that there was a dark side to Hannah's pregnancy.

In a time where pregnant girls were often sent to Magdalene asylums to avoid shame upon a family, Hannah's family appears to have been incredibly supportive. Was their motivation love and compassion, or were they protecting a secret? Could Betty have been the product of a familial incestuous encounter? What we know for sure is Hannah's family took care of her, arranged a home for her child and promptly sent her off to England. Later, they were proud to recount to local villagers Hannah's stories of a successful marriage and family abroad. My mother's biological father remains a mystery, and anyone who could shed light on the truth has long passed.

Sure, there were plenty of girls who got in trouble. (Betty Cummings)

While my father recalls that most young people toed the line, and avoided pre-marital sex, my mother insists in her village it was not uncommon for a couple to wed in order to legitimize a pregnancy. What could account for the difference in their perceptions: location, gender, or their individual experiences? My mother's village was far more insular than my father's; in fact, my mother recalls everyone was related, most having the surnames Carey or Golden. Her adoptive parents were distant cousins. Was life that different in the hills of Kerry? Or, perhaps as a woman, my mother would have been more aware of what was happening among her female peers. Finally, my mother's own illegitimate status may have led her to be more sensitive to the issue. Whatever the reasons for their dissimilar perceptions, it is clear that Ireland's harsh Catholicism and efforts to avoid acknowledging all things sexual, did not prevent the realities of sexuality, for better or for worse.

My mother posted her letter to her biological mother, returned home and cried on her bed through the night. Betty had a job lined up in Boston and she would need to get her passport and book her airplane ticket. But suddenly, her excitement and anticipation had turned to fear and anxiety. What if her friends and employers found out she was illegitimate when she got to America? Betty contemplated that her secret may not be a secret at all. In small villages everyone knew their neighbor's business. What if the friends who wrote to her about jobs in Boston already knew and were whispering behind her back? How, she thought, could Hannah's pregnancy have been kept a secret? Betty didn't know what she should do. Should she use her legal name, Golden, or introduce herself as Betty Carey? With her upcoming departure to America just months away, my mother had more questions than answers.

Kate advised her daughter to introduce herself as Betty Carey when she got to America. After all, she told her daughter, someday you'll get a husband and have a *real name*. Those words were not comforting to Betty. *What if,* she thought, *no man would marry a girl who didn't have a real name?*

Today, psychologists discuss the trauma that is often associated with adoption.[105] For my mother, she had to face the devastating news at precisely the time she needed the confidence to leave home for America. Adding to her insecurity was the secrecy that shrouded her identity. Betty's letter to Hannah may have provided her with a therapeutic release, but it could never have soothed the inner trauma she experienced. In the midst of her emotional hurricane, Betty had to secure her passport and make travel arrangements.

Kate had written her sister in America who would meet Betty at the airport and provide a temporary home until she settled into her new job. Kate assured her daughter that her aunt and her husband knew the truth about her adoption and were happy to welcome her. *Everything will be well,* she told Betty. But my mother quietly wondered if anything would ever be well again.

Betty consistently fought back tears when she reluctantly recounted this seminal time in her life. In an instant my mother had gone from being someone, a daughter who was part of the Carey family, to a young woman without a proper name, the product of a union between a *fallen woman* and unknown man, classified as *less than* by the political, social and religious structures that defined her world. There had been a point in Ireland's transition to an independent country when equality and opportunity for women as independent citizens had been a possibility. But those hopes had been buried by the time my mother was just a toddler.

---

[105] An excellent starting point on research surrounding adoption is, Brodzinsky, David, Marantz Heng, Robin, Schecter, Marshall, *Being Adopted: The Lifelong Search for Self.* NY, Random House, 1993.

During the early years of Ireland's fight for independence, equality for women was among the demands of Irish nationalists. The female revolutionaries who participated in the Easter Uprising of 1916, many of whom were socialists, envisioned an Ireland that stood apart from Great Britain and for women's suffrage, reproductive rights and gender equality. But feminism would be sacrificed on the altar of nationalism, and the free state of Ireland drafted a constitution that returned women to their traditional roles, celebrated for sexual purity in their unmarried state and glorified as mothers following their expected marriage nuptials.[106]

In crafting Ireland's 1937 Constitution de Valera sought the much-needed validation of the Catholic Church; and, in the process, absorbed their influence. As a result, the Irish Constitution, while guaranteeing female suffrage for women over 21 years of age, also included qualifying language allowing for gender policies that considered *differences of capacity, physical and moral, and of social function*.[107] The Irish Constitution was clear in its construction of the model of femininity.

In particular, the State recognizes that by her life within the home, woman gives to the State a support without which the common good cannot be achieved. The State shall, therefore, ensure that mothers shall not be obliged by economic necessity to engage in labour to the neglect of their duties in the home.[108]

My mother was born into a time where there was no question what constituted what it was to be righteous woman. Born of an illicit union, devalued by the world she lived in, Betty had to get

---

106 Lee, Mary Bridget. *Redefining Éireann: The Decline of Women's Rights in the Era of Irish Nationalism 1916-1937.* Doctoral Dissertation submitted to the Department of History, University of Michigan, 2015.
107 Bunreacht na hÉireann, 1937, Art. 40 via www.irishstatutebook.ie
108 Bunreacht na hÉireann, 1937, Art. 41.2 via www.irishstatutebook.ie

on a plane, fearful and ashamed. When it was to time for her to leave home, my mother packed her belongings into a suitcase Kate had purchased for her in town. Dan bit his lip as he hugged his daughter goodbye, and Kate could not hold back her tears as they flooded down her face. Betty kissed her parents, promised to write as soon as she arrived in America, and departed the hills of Kerry for America.

Betty left home clutching a new purse that her mother had bought for the trip. Inside the delicate bag was her passport, stamped Elizabeth Golden, also known as Elizabeth Carey. Believing her value lay solely in her future as a mother while wondering if any man would accept her, Betty may have arguably been the most frightened passenger on her flight to America.

CHAPTER FOURTEEN:
COOKIN', CLEANIN' AND LOOKIN' FOR A HUSBAND IN' BOSTON

I'd see the rats run across my bedroom. I couldn't wait to go upstairs to the main house. It was like leaving hell and going to heaven. (Betty Cummings)

A nineteen-year-old Elizabeth Golden, also known as Elizabeth Carey, arrived in Boston via airplane on April 6, 1953, and was met by her aunt, Kate's younger sister. Betty's aunt and her husband drove my mother to their home in Dorchester, which was just blocks away from where my dad would live when he came to Boston the following year. My mother told me she was in awe as she soaked up the energy of the city. It was, she said, as if *she was dropped on the moon.*

Betty stayed just two weeks with her aunt before moving in with her new employers. Through a series of written communications with other village girls, my mother had lined up a job working for a couple in Boston. For $30 a week, Betty cooked and cleaned for a Boston couple who owned an appliance store and lived a comfortable life in Boston's fashionable Back Bay neighborhood.

They were a childless, middle-aged couple, so my mother found the job quite easy compared to her previous position in Ireland where she had a family of five to attend.

While she found the work easy enough, Betty hated her bedroom, which was below grade. On more than one occasion my mother saw rats as they moved in and out of her basement room. Each morning, my mother would get up before dawn and head upstairs to the beautifully appointed brownstone's main floor. My mother told me it felt like she was leaving hell behind and going to heaven. After several months Betty looked for another position so she could escape her living conditions.

I asked my mother if she informed her employers about the rats, and she laughed. *Kathy, everyone knew there were rats in all the basements in Boston. It wasn't a fancy done-over room, but a make-shift bedroom near the furnace. Of course, they knew, but I was just a servant.* My mother also knew that as soon as she left, the couple would have another Irish girl in there in no time.

Betty was thrilled when she found a job paying $5 more each week cooking and cleaning for a Brookline family, a physician, his stay-at-home wife and three children. That the family was Jewish was new to my mother. Betty learned that observant Jews attended synagogue on Saturday and did not celebrate Christmas. But as she said, *we believed in the same God, just in different ways.* My mother had fond memories of the kindness and caring shown to her by the doctor and his wife. Betty told me they made her feel like a *real person,* and not just a servant.

My mother explained that at one point she was quite sick with a fever and sore throat, and she said nothing, continuing to cook and clean. Her boss noticed she wasn't well, and when she asked Betty how she was feeling she was shocked that Betty had said nothing of her illness. *My goodness Betty,* she said, *my husband is a doctor, he'll help you. You only need to ask.* My mother told her boss that she didn't want to be a bother, but she insisted that all my mother needed to do was to ask—anytime—and they would gladly help.

The doctor examined my mother and gave her an antibiotic, giving her two days off to rest. Betty was overwhelmed when on pay day, the doctor and his wife gave her a full week's salary. She expected they would deduct wages for the two days they gave her to recuperate. *I was speechless,* Betty said, *I couldn't believe their generosity.*

My mother told me she had never known such kindness as a servant. Unlike her position in the Boston's Back Bay where her bedroom was in the basement, Betty had a *proper* bedroom in the Brookline home on the first floor, off the kitchen. She also told me the lady of the house would on occasion, sit in the kitchen with her and have a cup of tea. My mother was shocked that her boss would ask her questions about life in Ireland, and that she actually seemed interested to hear her answers.

Like my father, my mother saw the world as a place which housed the rich and everyone else. *Everyone else* had to work hard, defer to the rich and never expect anything more than what you earned. Betty was in disbelief that this Brookline couple who had all the power, cared enough to pay her sick leave and treat her with respect. My mother told me that experience helped her believe that maybe someday she could have something *more.*

While Betty loved working for the doctor and his wife in Brookline, she soon was asked to accept a position at a Catholic parish in Charlestown. The parish was looking for someone who could both cook and clean and a parishioner and friend suggested my mother. Betty felt, as a devout Catholic, she could never say no to a representative of God on earth and she accepted the position. Betty told the Brookline couple how much she had enjoyed working for them and assured them she would never have accepted another position had it not been the church who was asking. She also gave them a list of Irish girls who, she knew, would love the job.

Begrudgingly, Betty left the Brookline family to move into Saint Mary's Parish Rectory near the Bunker Hill Monument in Charlestown. There, she cooked and cleaned for the parish priests. My mother said it took her a bit of time to get used to seeing priests as *ordinary people.* But in time Betty became more comfortable, and as she pointed out *the work and the schedule were always the same.*

Irish girls in service consistently worked the same schedules in Boston; they had two partial days off, Thursday and Sunday, after making breakfast for their families. My mother had a group of friends, all of whom were in service to affluent Boston area families. A few were from her village and others came from throughout Ireland. Together, they shopped, socialized and hoped to meet their future husbands.

We'd try on lipsticks and face powder and get ice cream. Those were happy days. (Betty Cummings)

One of my mother's happiest memories during that time was joining her friends to go downtown to shop at Jordan Marsh. The department store opened in downtown Boston in 1841 and when my mother arrived, it was, as she said, *the place to shop.* Unlike what Betty called the *posh* shops on Boston's Newbury Street,

Jordan Marsh offered a variety of clothing and accessories at various price points.[109]

Betty's favorite section of the store was the makeup counter, which offered samples and was staffed by knowledgeable women who assisted her in makeup application. Putting on *a face* was a new concept to my mother since makeup was nonexistent in her Irish village. She and her friends would try on different shades of lipstick, rouge and powders. And Betty quickly learned that a woman never left home without a lipstick and face powder compact in her purse.

Every trip in town was always finished off with a treat, which might be an ice cream cone or one of Jordan Marsh's famous blueberry muffins. The young women would walk Boston Common, and especially during the Christmas season, enjoy the bright lights and annual enchanted village display. In the summer, they frequently rode the swan boats in Boston's Public Gardens. Public transportation was inexpensive and widely available throughout the city, so joining up with friend was easy, and always a delight.

My mother lit up when she described the fun she had with her female friends in town. When she had children in later years, she regularly took my sisters and me into town on the train to see holiday lights and to enjoy a special sweet treat. Looking back, Betty was likely revisiting those happy memories as she created new ones with her daughters.

But more than shopping trips, Betty and her friends were interested in meeting available young men. Since domestics

---

109 Jordan Marsh was bought out by Macys in the 1990s. The chain store suffered from suburban expansion and the advent of the mall. Good starting points for department store history include *The Department Store Museum* at http://www.thedepartmentstoremuseum.org/2010/09/jordan-marsh-company-boston.html. For Jordan Marsh specifically see https://www.cbsnews.com/boston/news/bostons-lost-landmarks-jordan-marsh-downtown-crossing/.

were off on Thursday, the Irish halls in Boston hosted dances on Thursday evenings to bring young men and women together. After *putting on her face,* Betty joined her friends and headed to Dudley Street in the Roxbury section of Boston where the biggest Irish dances were held.[110] Here, recent Irish immigrants looked for future mates as they danced the night away. My mother met and dated a few Irish men, but nothing came of it until she met Larry Kilcommins, her future husband, in 1956. At the time they met, my mother had been in America nearly three years, and my father, nearly two.

He asked to bring me home after the dance. Of course, that meant riding the train with me. No one had a car back then. (Betty Cummings)

My father told me that he was immediately attracted to my mother, whom he regarded as quite pretty. Betty was a slender 5'5" with blue eyes and wavy hair that had transformed from childhood blonde to light brown. After asking her to dance multiple times the evening they met, Larry offered to bring her home. Together, they rode public transportation to my mother's Charlestown residence, and he asked her for her phone number after walking her to the door. Dates continued every week at the dance, although from that point on, she became his sole partner. Weekly dances, the occasional Sunday movie, and on rare—and special occasions—a dinner out, continued for a full year. After a year of dating, my father began the discussion of marriage, and my mother was terrified.

I wanted to tell him, but I was so afraid he'd run off. (Betty Cummings)

---

110 See again, Gedutis, *See You at the Hall: Boston's Golden Era of Irish Music and Dance.*

As my parents' relationship moved from dating to a committed relationship each understood that marriage was on the horizon. My mother told me she wanted to tell my father about her illegitimate status many times but couldn't bring herself to do so. She was frightened that he would *run off* the minute he knew. On the one-year anniversary of the evening he met Betty, Larry said he'd like to buy her a diamond ring. And Betty burst into tears.

She told my dad about her birth mother and how she had just learned the truth right before leaving for America. Larry handed Betty his handkerchief to wipe away her tears and hugged her. While my father was kind and said he loved my mother all the same, he also told her that he had to discuss the situation with his family, especially his brother Mike.

As the eldest brother, Mike continued to hold a great deal of authority over his siblings, as he had in Ireland. Larry met with his siblings at Mary's home in Dorchester on a Sunday afternoon and shared my mother's story. My Aunt Mary was the first to declare that my mother had *no blame or shame,* since it was all beyond her control. Mike concurred and firmly endorsed the engagement. With his siblings' approval, my mother and father announced their engagement.

I have often wondered what my father would have done had his engagement not been approved by his eldest brother. I suspect he would not have gone through with the wedding. While love is a powerful emotion, for the rural Irish at that time, doing what was right, and approved by your family, was a more powerful force.

I, Lawrence Francis take you, Elizabeth for my lawful wife, to have and to hold from this day forward, for better, for worse, for richer, for poorer, in sickness and health, until death do us part. (Larry Cummings)

Larry and Betty married on June 1, 1957, at the church where my mother worked. It was a small affair; my mother wore a borrowed dress, and they returned to my Aunt Mary's house for sandwiches, tea and cake. They had decided that rather than have a larger wedding, they would use their savings to return to Ireland for the summer.

Together they had been diligent savers, a quality each appreciated in the other. At the time of their marriage, their combined bank accounts totaled $7000, Betty had saved $3000 and Larry $4000. Not an insignificant amount, in today's dollars their combined savings would equal $76,000.[111] The lion's share of their savings was spent on what they regarded as a *once in a lifetime honeymoon*.

Larry and Betty enjoyed a three-week journey aboard a ship that took them from New York to Ireland. They spent another six weeks in Ireland and returned by ship for the final leg of their honeymoon journey. From early June through late August Betty and Larry honeymooned, were introduced to their in-laws, and reconnected with friends and family who had stayed in Ireland.

Their first destination was my mother's home in Kerry. After arriving by train in Killorglin, they took a taxi to my mother's childhood home where she saw her parents for the first time in just over four years. It was a tearful, joyous reunion, and my grandmother presented my mother with a family heirloom, a set of six sterling teaspoons as a wedding present. I am honored to have those spoons in my possession today.

Mike told him to make sure the place was cleaned and looked good for Betty. (Betty Cummings)

---

111   The figure uses an inflation calculator from the Bureau of Labor Statistics, using 1957 as compared to 2023.

After spending a week visiting with my mother's parents, my father took a train alone to his home in Galway. My Uncle Mike was concerned that there were no longer girls at home with his aging parents, and the house might not be fit for company. He instructed my father to go on alone and make sure the house was clean and presentable for my mother's arrival. My father did exactly what his oldest brother instructed and headed to Galway to prepare the home for my mother's introduction.

Jesus, he was up at dawn and on the tractor in front of the house. He couldn't wait to get started. (Paddy Kilcommins)

While my mother enjoyed time alone with her mother, my father's youngest brother Paddy was thrilled to have my dad back on the farm. He recalls that the morning after his arrival my father was up at dawn and sitting up on a recent purchase, the first tractor in the Kilcommins family, calling out for Paddy to get out of bed and join him in the day's chores. My dad worked all day, every day, during his honeymoon, while staying with his family. And his kid brother Paddy was grateful for his help. Larry worked on his honeymoon, not out of a sense of duty, or as a favor, rather he worked the farm because he loved it. There is no doubt he missed life in Ireland, and he would spend much of his honeymoon doing what he had always loved, farming.

My grandmother would have watched my dad at work and recalled all the days they worked the fields together. Nora would have recalled the fateful fight between my father and grandfather and his expulsion from the family home. And now he had briefly returned, married, with a life in Boston, and yet he farmed daily and with passion. Nora watched the son who was ordered to leave, and would have given anything to stay, ride up to the front of her home, anxious to get to the farm, and calling up to the son who would inherit the farm that he never wanted.

My father stayed a week before returning to Kerry to pick up my mother, a trip he made in yet another recent Kilcommins purchase, a car. Without a brood of children to feed and senior pensions from the government, life had become easier at the Kilcommins home. Machinery replaced bodies and both a tractor and car were available to the youngest son left at home, though Paddy always wished it had been my father in his stead.

My parents went back and forth between Kerry and Galway, meeting their in-laws and visiting with extended family and friends. My mother recalls especially liking her father-in-law Paddy, though she found her mother-in-law Nora to be a bit bossy. Interestingly, this was the same complaint my grandmother Nora had about her mother-in-law. My father recalls his mother-in-law Kate as one of the kindest women he had ever met. Larry and Betty concluded their trip where it began, in Kerry. Betty kissed her mother and father goodbye, promising to return with a family again someday. But Betty would never see her mother again. By the time my parents would save enough to return to Ireland, Kate would be dead.

Betty and Larry concluded their honeymoon aboard the return ship to New York and looked forward to settling into their new home in Dorchester. My mother was quite happy that she had a *"real name"* and was especially excited since she suspected she might be pregnant. My father was proud of his new wife and their new life, though there was a part of him that deeply wished they could raise their family in Ireland. The couple returned home to Boston and the confirmation that Betty was expecting their first child. It was, my mother told me, *the happiest time of their lives.*

CHAPTER FIFTEEN:
BUILDING A FAMILY WITHOUT A SAFETY NET

The Irish in Boston started their American married lives on the foundations established in Ireland: hard work, traditional gender boundaries, and strict Catholicism. Men went to work, many found jobs through the connections of Irish immigrants who had come before them, and women had babies. Certainly, some women made extra money by doing occasional cleaning, or taking in boarders, but men were traditionally the breadwinners. This was especially true since babies came soon after a marriage, and most couples had multiple children as they did back home in Ireland.

The Irish tended to settle in the Dorchester area of Boston where they joined local Irish-Catholic parishes, sent their children to parish schools and socialized with other Irish. Like my parents, many started off renting a small flat and then saved a down payment to buy a multi-family home, often a three-decker. The goal was to someday move to the suburbs, a place they regarded as safe, comfortable and an ideal setting to raise a family. It seemed for working-class Irish, life was about waiting for the next place, and all their next destination promised. From the farm to America, from the city to the suburbs, the Irish were living for tomorrow. But getting to their final destination was not easy and like most immigrants, it encompassed hard work, sacrifice and sadly, sometimes tragedy.

My father's eldest sister Mary and her husband Ben lost their second child, a daughter, to sudden infant death syndrome when she was just weeks old. They had to borrow money to bury her in the local parish cemetery. My Aunt's pain was still apparent more than 60 years later when she recounted her baby's death. It took her and her husband a year to save the money to repay the cost of their daughter's funeral. For my father and his siblings there was no financial safety net; they had to rely on their own capacity to work, earn and save. And in America, it all seemed possible.

If you wanted work, you could work. (Larry Cummings)

My parents, and other Irish immigrants in the 1950s, benefited from the *boom generation.* Post-war America saw an economic boom, a baby boom, and expansion of interstate highways, schools and suburban growth.[112] With plenty of working-class jobs available to an uneducated populace, there was more than enough opportunity to go around. Unlike immigrants today who are confronted with a contraction of unskilled labor jobs that pay a living wage, such jobs abounded for immigrants in the 1950s. Although my parents and their peers did not have familial safety nets, the parents who *helped you get started,* they did have opportunity. And they embraced it.

---

[112] A brief summary is available at http://www.history.com/topics/1950s.

Larry continued his position as a janitor at Harvard University and worked any side job that came his way. He and Betty settled into a small apartment on Draper Street in Dorchester and welcomed their first child into the world, my sister Noreen who was named for my dad's mother. I followed a year later and was named for the woman who raised my mother, Kate.

In the same year, my father proudly became an American citizen, though Betty would never pursue citizenship and ultimately died still a legal alien. I suspect the humiliation of having to produce her birth certificate was too emotionally painful for my mother. Betty chose to retreat from her past by not confronting it. She had a *real* name now as Mrs. Larry Cummings and that was enough for her. She and my dad remained on Draper Street for two years until they had saved a down payment on a three-decker on Templeton Street, also in Dorchester.[113]

Three deckers were built in central New England industrial cities between 1870-1910 to accommodate a rapidly expanding immigrant population. While in cities like New York, where immigrants crowded into cramped, often windowless tenements, wooden three-deckers offered large, airy rooms with heat and hot water. Three deckers often provided immigrants with a pathway to suburban home ownership since two floors could be rented, offsetting housing costs, allowing the family to save for a single-family suburban home.[114]

Irish immigrants, like my parents, frequently continued the tradition of purchasing three deckers. My parents were now

---

113   In the current real estate market (2023), many three-deckers where my parents first settled have been converted to condominiums. With access to public transportation and a quick commute to downtown Boston, these condos sell at a premium.

114   See, The Rise, Fall, and Rebirth of the Three Decker, NewEnglandHistoricalSociety. com (2014).

landlords and rented the two apartments above them as my father acquired home improvement skills, through trial-and-error, and through the instruction of other Irish immigrants. A number of their Irish peers purchased more than one, accumulating real estate holdings that in a few cases turned into considerable wealth. My parents, however, had saved enough to head to the suburbs when my younger sister, Lynda, arrived in 1962.

Now a family of five, the small three-decker apartment was starting to close in on our family. My parents made the decision to sell the property, knowing that many of the cosmetic improvements my father had made to the home would increase its value. Since they couldn't afford a popular South Shore community, Milton, where a number of my father's siblings lived, they headed farther south to Braintree.

In 1963 the Cummings family moved into a small 3-bedroom, 1-bathroom, Cape-style home with a one car garage, under the house, and a good-sized back yard. For $17,000 they had purchased their dream home. Six years later, my brother Larry Jr. was born, and the Cummings family had reached its full size.

Our neighborhood, like the overwhelming majority of the town, was exclusively white and primarily housed working class families. All of the families on our street embraced traditional gender roles where women remained at home and men went to work. Every family owned a single car and a single, black-and-white television. My parents were the only immigrants though others were second or third generation in their families. Everyone in the neighborhood was Christian, and whether Protestant or Catholic, all regularly attended services.

As young children we went to Mass every Sunday, attended the local parochial school and aside from neighborhood friends, largely associated with our extended Irish relatives. With the exception of my Uncle Tom who never had children, my father and his siblings in America, Mike, John, Mary and Peggy, produced a total of twenty-four children. As young children we routinely spent holidays together and enjoyed family barbeques. Like most American children, we went in our own directions as adolescence approached. But prior to adolescence, and before my brother was born, my parents brought us *home* to Ireland for a three-week summer vacation.

Nearly every Irish immigrant saved for the once-in-a-lifetime trip home with their children. My sisters and I were quite excited, since we had never been beyond New England, and had never been on an airplane. Looking back, it seems counterintuitive that my mother would take us shopping to buy fancy suits to wear on the plane. We were traveling late at night and would sleep on the plane, and comfortable clothing certainly made more sense. But air travel in the mid-1960s was a big deal for working-class families, and my mother was intent that we would be well-dressed and arrive in Ireland in style.

My sisters and I stepped off the plane in Shannon Airport in the summer of 1967 wearing our fancy suits, gloves and carrying our pocketbooks. We had loved the plane ride and I recall thinking the food on Aer Lingus was delicious. My father enjoyed more than one complimentary nip of Irish Mist and we all regarded the trip as a great adventure.

My Uncle Paddy met us at the airport, and I found him to be a kind, funny man who looked thrilled to see my dad again. We drove several hours to the Kilcommins family home, and I recall thinking I had never seen so many shades of green. It was a beautiful country and at every stop, people were both friendly and curious. My sisters and I were referred to as the *Yankee girls*, and when we stopped, we were offered candies and orange soda. My mother had brought a bag of Kennedy half-dollars and every time we were given a treat, she presented the American souvenir, which was always received with grateful reverence.

When we finally arrived at my father's home, we were introduced to my grandparents. I found my grandfather to be a kind, interesting man, and my grandmother to be a bit grumpy. She was clearly delighted to see my father, but I got the sense she would have preferred that he come alone.

My Uncle Paddy was quite proud to show us that the house now had internal plumbing, which had been installed the year before we arrived. There was a bathroom with a toilet, sink, and small shower, and the kitchen had running water. I remember I found it odd that a bathroom should be such a point of pride, but I got the sense that I should act impressed. Since there were still just two bedrooms, my parents and siblings and I occupied the bedroom where my father and his brothers had been as children. My parents slept in what had been his grandparents' bed and my sisters and I slept in the bed my father had occupied with his brothers. My uncle was also proud to tell us that the beds had real mattresses now, and not the hay-stuffed sacks that they had slept on as kids. I quickly learned I would need to act impressed at what to me, seemed just the way things should be.

I recall not enjoying my dad's family farm; it was dirty, and animals seemed to roam freely among people. I recall being frightened by the chickens that I found a bit aggressive. I was struck that my father seemed to absolutely love it, and I found it odd that he should spend a vacation working on the farm. But he was happy and as children, my sisters and I did enjoy the horse drawn wagon rides to which my uncle treated us several times. We traveled throughout the village in our American clothes, and villagers all turned out to meet the *Yankee girls*. My father treated local villagers to drinks at the local pub, and my sisters and I sat with my mother and other women in the back room. Gender still divided the rural Irish, and it was not lost on me as a young girl that it seemed odd. But each time, we were given an orange soda that we found delicious, and the Irish candy was rich and creamy and always appreciated.

I lived on Irish orange soda and candy during the trip. Milk still came directly from the cow, and I spit my first taste across the table, resulting in a stern look of disapproval from my father. All the food seemed inedible to me, and I tended to just move it around on my plate, longing for American-style food.

After a week at my father's, we traveled in a rental car to my mother's home in Kerry. I thought the Ring of Kerry must be the most beautiful place in the world. If there had been a Garden of Eden, I believed it would be in Kerry. My mother's small cottage was just the way it had been in her childhood. Her mother had passed and her father, Dan, remained with no desire to incorporate modern conveniences. There was no bathroom and no running water within the cottage. In anticipation, my mother had packed toilet tissue and we would each be given a few sheets to go outside *behind the bush,* an event I found disgusting.

Neighbors came each night we stayed, and they sipped whiskey from the bottles my dad brought as gifts, as they chatted around the fire. I was struck that with no television and no radio, people placed chairs in a semi-circle around the hearth and talked, laughed, and told stories. They seemed so happy, and I think that was the first time that I realized happiness is not contingent on material wealth.

My grandfather was a talented topiarist and I loved walking through the shrubberies he had carved into animals and other interesting shapes. For a child, it allowed a wonderful space to let your imagination go and play. He also had a donkey that was kept in a small corral. Every time I approached the fence the donkey slowly moved toward me, and I patted him. I recall thinking it was such a sweet pet.

One evening I thought the donkey might enjoy a bite of my pink candy stick. Long, pink solid candy sticks were frequent gifts to my sisters and me when we went into town. I pulled down the plastic wrapping about an inch and offered it over the fence to my new pet. I was horrified when the donkey grabbed the whole stick and ate it, plastic and all. I ran into the cottage and in front of all the neighbors gathered around the hearth yelled out, *I am so sorry, I wanted to share my candy with the donkey, but he ate the whole thing with the plastic on it. Will he get sick?* The entire room burst into hysterical laughter. My grandfather walked over, patted me on the back, and told me not to worry, the donkey would be just fine. And I am certain that I provided a humorous story for the neighbors when they moved on to another *chat around the hearth.*

We returned to my father's home and at the conclusion of our three-week vacation, my Uncle Paddy drove us to the airport. My parents were quiet through most of the ride, and my father, in particular, looked quite sad. It was the first time I saw my father cry. He hugged his brother as they both wept.

Years later when I returned to Ireland with my son and nephew, my Uncle Paddy told me that when our family had visited those many years ago, the farm next to him was for sale. He had begged my father to buy it and raise our family in Ireland. Paddy would have a sibling and my father could do what he loved. My father went to see the farm and Paddy said he eagerly embraced the idea, but my mother would not hear of it. Paddy told me he was quite sad when my mother sternly informed my father that *there is nothing for your daughters here.* As our family boarded our plane for Boston's Logan International Airport, my father was again in mourning. It was the second time he would lose his dream.

We returned home and to my parents' desire to recreate an environment for their children that was reminiscent of their childhoods in Ireland. But it was not to be. My mother didn't want to live in Ireland, but she didn't want to raise children in what she came to regard as the chaos of America either. The 1960s exploded with new music, new ideas, and a younger generation with a fresh perspective on everything from politics to sex, to drugs, and to family values. I will never know for sure, but I have to believe that on more than one occasion, my father would have reminded my mother that they should have bought that farm next to his brother and raised their children in Ireland.

CHAPTER SIXTEEN:
WORLDS APART: RAISING CHILDREN IN THE ERA OF SEX, DRUGS AND ROCK'N ROLL

Every Irish family had his picture on the wall, right next to the Pope, and the Last Supper. (Betty Cummings)

It began with such hope and inspiration for the Irish in America—one of *their own* had been elected president in 1961. President Kennedy's image hung on our living room wall, right next to the image of the Pope, and a 3-dimensional rendering of the Last Supper. They were the requisite images for every Irish family, and they reflected their strong Catholic beliefs, and their overwhelming pride that their president was Irish-Catholic. John Kennedy, a product of wealth and ivy-league education had little in common with the uneducated, working-class Irish that adored him. But he had Irish roots, and he was the first Catholic president, and that was all they needed to know to support him.

Kennedy had promised a *New Frontier,* an America that ended injustice and inequality. An inspirational leader, he instructed

Americans: *Ask not what your country can do for you--ask what you can do for your country.* In the process he inspired the Peace Corps, the space program, and an America where every citizen, regardless of race, had access to opportunity. His assassination gave rise to President Johnson's *Great Society,* which made strides in civil rights and gave birth to the *War against Poverty.* But as America moved in a new direction, the slow pace frustrated a younger generation, who were anxious for meaningful and sustained reform. Citizens of color demanded fair treatment and access; women demanded equality, and the children of the Baby Boom generation now looked suspiciously upon elected officials who had increasingly involved them in the Vietnam conflict.[115]

Sure, they were shameless—burn'in their bras! (Larry Cummings)

As the country erupted during the tumultuous 1960s with a series of riots and protests, newly arrived working-class Irish watched their black and white TV sets each night in bewildered amazement. For my father, who personally witnessed Harvard University protests,[116] he was incredulous that a younger generation could be so disrespectful, so ungrateful, and so *shameless* in their reckless behavior. To his mind, these were spoiled, rich kids who had way too much time on their hands.

For Irish, like my father, who had been raised to respect authority, work hard, and be grateful for their opportunities in America, this was a generation they could not understand, and nor would they try. In particular, female protesters challenged not

---

115 For an enjoyable and informative read on the 1960s see, William O'Neill's *Coming Apart: An Informal History of America in the 1960s.* Quandrangle Press, Chicago, 1971.
116 See Roger Rosenblatt's *Coming Apart: A Memoir of the Harvard Wars of 1969,* Little, Little and Brown, Boston, 1997.

only their ideas of order and respect for authority, but the central relationships that shaped their worlds. While the *bra-burning* stories were more apocryphal than reality,[117] they represented an era of fundamental change in gender relations. Irish parents felt unsettled as they lived in a society with which they could not identify and could never embrace. And yet their children were in the thick of it.

As children of immigrant parents in the 1960s we benefited from three key realties; our parents were white, spoke English, and had easily immigrated legally to America. We did not face the challenges and discrimination that children of color faced, or children who lived in homes where English was not the primary language. Nor did we face the challenges of families with parents who had immigrated illegally. My siblings, cousins and I also had access to decent public high schools, and many of us went on to college. But, consistently, our parents regarded their Catholic faith as the most important legacy that they could give their children.

Our parents brought all of us to Sunday Mass, and most of us attended parochial elementary schools. But Catholicism has not remained a central defining force in the most of our lives. In my family, only my brother is a practicing Catholic; my sisters and I long ago parted with the Catholic Church. Patterns are similar among my aunts and uncles' families. While our parents were raised to obey and respect authority and to accept the tenets of the Catholic Church without question, we were raised in an era where challenging authority was the norm.

Shaped by the Watergate scandal, the aftermath of the Vietnam War, and the Civil Rights and Women's Movements, we

---

[117] See https://www.snopes.com/history/american/burnbra.asp.

did question our parents' values. As a consequence, we would lead very different lives from our immigrant parents. While my parents socialized exclusively with Irish-Catholic friends and relations, we moved into a world that embraced the increasing complexity of American life. Our parents lived within their comfort level; but as children, we redefined comfort to conform to a new world that included new political, social, sexual, and intellectual pursuits.

I witnessed my parents struggle with many issues that were foreign to them, but the new norm in their children's lives, including pre-marital sex, divorce, non-traditional gender roles and rejection of Catholicism. Interestingly, while all of my father's siblings dealt with the same issues with their children, the tactic among my uncles and aunts was one of silence. Defined by the shame and guilt that had shaped their upbringing in rural Ireland, no sibling wanted to confess to another that his or her child was getting divorced, *living in sin,* or rejecting Catholicism. It was as if they felt by not publicly owning it, they could create a "truth" that remained consistent with their values.

As time went on, however, and our parents entered their senior years, they lost the need to hide the perceived shame of their children. Age had forced them to accept the world as it had become. Irish American families are as American today as children born to native parents. For good or for bad, our divorce rate, addiction rate, and college graduation rate are consistent with national averages. Some are Democrats, but as many are Republicans or Independents. We occupy different steps on the financial ladder. In short, we are assimilated Americans, very different from our parents who came across the pond to start new lives.

My parents could not create and sustain in America the Irish-Catholic, structured, and predictable world they left behind.

Their journeys across the pond had left that world permanently in their pasts. For my parents, they struggled with parenting as their children moved into their adolescent years. The early years, however, when the children were in elementary school, were easier for them.

Although my father spoke of the pains of corporal punishment as a child, he no less used the same on his own children. The strap was his preferred instrument for severe transgressions. Lessons were quickly learned, however, and we understood that we needed to either obey or keep our transgressions secret. Consistent with her upbringing, my mother never used physical punishment and often hid our disobedience from my father to protect us. She would often say, *next time, I will tell your father when he gets home,"* though she rarely did.

My children have asked me if I regarded my father's use of the strap as child abuse. While by today's standards it would qualify as such, it is important and prudent to judge actions within the time period that they occurred. I went to a parochial elementary school where the nuns used a ruler to slap students who talked during a lesson, chewed gum or passed a note in class. In the neighborhood where I grew up, all of the parents employed corporal punishment. The United States Supreme Court upheld the use of corporal punishment in schools as late as 1977, the year I graduated from high school.[118] Popular culture similarly reinforced the notion that parental discipline and the use of corporal punishment was acceptable, even desirable.[119] And while

---

118 Oluwole, Joseph. *"Ingraham v. Wright".* Encyclopedia Britannica, 12 Apr. 2022, https://www.britannica.com/event/Ingraham-v-Wright. Accessed 8 March 2023.
119 A simple Google search using *"television programs and corporal punishment"* will display programs by decade. There were many when I was growing up in the 1960s and 1970s.

my parents regarded the need to *keep their children in line* to be the first priority, it was followed closely by the need to instill a work ethic.

Throughout our childhood years, my siblings and I were assigned both daily and weekly chores. We were expected to make our beds and wash and dry dishes on a daily basis, and thoroughly clean our rooms and hang out laundry on a weekly basis. Our home didn't have a dishwasher or clothes dryer until the mid-1970s, luxuries that we all received with great excitement. In addition, we shoveled snow in the winter months, cut the lawn and raked during the spring, summer and fall seasons. But more than doing chores and being well-behaved, each child was expected to accept the tenets of Catholicism without question.

Each night we knelt beside our beds as my father led us in prayer, and each Sunday we filed into the pew as an orderly, well-dressed family. Going to weekly mass was an event in our home, and we were expected to wear our *Sunday best* clothing. Each girl was dressed in a hat, dress, ankle socks and shiny patent leather shoes. On Easter Sunday, we were also given white gloves and a small purse. By the time my brother came along, the dress code was more relaxed, but in the early years, my parents insisted we show *proper respect* in God's house. I loved dressing up on Sunday, but I struggled with the tacit acceptance of Catholicism from an early age, and my father, in particular, struggled with his response to me. It was during a dinner with our local parish priest that things came to a head.

Father Cullinane was in our local parish, Saint Thomas More Church in Braintree, just eleven miles south of Boston. Catholic parishes flourished at the time, and he was one of three priests. My father loved his sermons, and we would consistently attend masses that Father Cullinane conducted. Father Cullinane was among the first generation of Irish immigrant parents, and he was outgoing, eloquent and humorous. Laughing during a Sunday homily was a rare treat, and my father looked forward to the experience each week. After mass, my father would strike up a conversation with Father and their chats eventually led to an invitation to dinner. At eleven years of age, I will never forget the preparation that preceded Father Cullinane's visit.

My older sister, Noreen and I were charged with cleaning the house, and my father had given us strict orders that it were to be *immaculate*. My mother shopped for an expensive roast beef, and ironed cloth napkins. My father bought the most expensive whiskey that our local liquor store carried. My mother had her hair done at the local beauty shop, and we were all dressed in our Sunday best outfits. My mother helped my father pick out the right tie, since he was color blind and always had difficulty pulling an outfit together. My siblings and I were told to say, *Hello Father,* and then remain quiet through the rest of the evening. We were to eat dinner together and then go to our bedrooms, leaving my parents to entertain Father Cullinane in the living room. The tension in the house was palpable and when the doorbell rang my family quickly formed a welcoming line as my father opened the door.

Hello Father, we sang out in unison as our parish priest walked through the door. My father was beaming with pride that we should have a priest in our home for dinner and invited Father Cullinane into the living room for a glass of whiskey before dinner. I recall he asked for it *neat,* an unfamiliar phrase to me. But my father quickly poured a generous amount of whiskey into one of our *fancy* glasses and walked into the living room to talk with Father.

My siblings and I stayed in the kitchen with my mother and about twenty minutes later, she announced that dinner was ready. We said grace, and then my mother nervously brought the roast beef to the table telling Father that she hoped it was cooked the way he liked it. Graciously, Father Cullinane responded that it looked just perfect, and my mother beamed. As instructed, my siblings and I did not speak, until Father Cullinane directed the conversation to me.

As a student at the parish elementary school, I attended mass the first Friday of each month with the entire student body. After the homily, the priest would walk down between the pews and ask the students questions. The previous week, Father Cullinane had queried our student body and he told me how impressed he was that I always had my hand up and readily answered questions correctly. My father looked quite pleased with Father's praise until the conversation continued. *You must enjoy your catechism class, Kathy, since you always seem to have the right answers,* he commented. *Actually, Father, I know the answers because I study them, but I have some difficulty with some of the teachings,* I replied. My parents looked as if an earthquake had just happened, and Father Cullinane looked intrigued. *Give me an example, Kathy,* he replied. And then the earthquake turned into a tsunami.

Well, Father, I continued, *let's start with the story of Adam and Eve. If the human species truly started in a garden and Adam and Eve were the first man and woman, then all future humans would have to have been the result of incest. It just doesn't make sense to me.* The blood drained from my father's face and my mother's jaw dropped. My father tried to get a few words out and apologize before Father Cullinane continued. *Kathy, do you know what a metaphor is?* he asked. *Yes, Father, I do.* I answered. *Good,* he continued, *because most of the Bible is a series of metaphors designed to teach us lessons. The majority of the stories are not true. And, you are right, the human species did not start in the Garden of Eden, but life did start in the Middle East. We use the story of Adam and Eve to teach children that God started life, and there is right and wrong. The Garden of Eden is a metaphor.*

My parents were incredulous. They believed in the literal interpretation of the Bible and had never questioned what they had been taught. The instant anger they felt at my comments gave way to what must have been feelings of bewildered awe and confusion. I thanked Father Cullinane for his thoughtful response and told him that made more sense to me.

After dessert, my siblings and I went to our bedrooms and my parents went into the living room with Father. Our house was small, and sound easily traveled. I heard my father say to our priest that he didn't know what to do with me sometimes, but Father Cullinane told my parents a curious mind was a good thing. I recall feeling that while there was a lot about my catechism class I questioned, I liked Father Cullinane.

That I understood the meaning of incest in early adolescence was not a product of parental instruction about sex education. I had my first menstruation when I barely turned eleven, and my parents had never discussed sex with me or my siblings. The evening I first menstruated my father and mother sat me down in the living room after telling my sisters to go upstairs, and my father said, *you know you are a woman now, and you can get pregnant.* I responded, yes. *Good,* he said, *and if you ever get pregnant, I'll kill you.* While I knew my father didn't mean it in the literal sense, I fully appreciated that getting pregnant was the worst thing that a girl could possibly do.

That exchange was my only discussion about sex with my parents. I quickly learned that to understand what was happening I had to rely on information from peers and older girls, as well as research in the library. An avid reader, I loved the library and found with a little research, I could learn a great deal about subjects my parents would never openly discuss with their children.

Larry and Betty never felt it was their responsibility to educate their children about sex. Their parents had not done so for them, and they felt no obligation to do so for their children. Just as in Ireland, they continued to regard anything sexual as off-limits, not to be discussed. I recall an innocent event that turned into a hysteria of sorts when my younger sister, Lynda, first learned to read.

Sunday dinner was a tradition in my home growing up. The menu was always the same, well-done roast beef, potatoes, and soggy vegetables. Most Irish overcooked whatever protein they prepared, cooked vegetables to the point of nearly liquifying them, and added either mashed or baked potato as a starch. To add flavor, everything was covered in salt and butter. My mother was busy preparing our Sunday traditional fare while my younger sister Lynda was in the bathroom reading labels on boxes in the linen closet.

Lynda had just learned to read, and she was absorbing anything she could find. In the bathroom, she found a box that read *Feminine Napkins*. Excited to find fancy napkins in the bathroom, Lynda decided to surprise our family at dinner by placing them on the dining room table. She snuck into the small dining room, which had a closed door to the kitchen, and placed a feminine napkin under each fork. In those days feminine napkins were thick pads with more than two inches of gauze fabric at each end to tie into a belt that young women wore during menstruation. Lynda was so happy to view the dining table as each fork rested on top of more than two inches of the fancy napkins she had found in the bathroom.

My mother announced that dinner was ready, and we marched into the dining room in our Sunday best outfits. My father shrieked as he viewed the menstrual pads. Anyone listening would have thought someone were breaking into our home, or someone were found dead on the floor. My mother ran from the dining room, put the roast on the kitchen counter and quickly removed the menstrual pads from her Sunday table. My father left for the living room where he ate his dinner alone on a TV tray, and my sisters and I sat with my mother in silence in the kitchen. Lynda was disappointed and confused as no one explained what was so wrong in her effort to do something *fancy* for Sunday dinner. Just like in Ireland, in our home, when it came to things sexual, *the less said about it, the better.*

It was challenging for two parents who had been raised in an insular world and remained cocooned in an Irish-Catholic dominated lifestyle, to understand the world in which their children were growing up. While the Internet was decades away, compared to the world in which Larry and Betty had been raised, information exchange was exploding. As children, my siblings and I had access to television, libraries and an educational system that presented the complexities of the newly emerging post-modern world. Larry and Betty had grave difficulty coming to terms with modern America, and their children's place in it.

CHAPTER SEVENTEEN:
YOU'RE NOT IN IRELAND ANYMORE

You know Larry, President Lincoln freed the slaves. (Mary Finneran, Larry's sister)

Throughout his life Larry was characterized by all who knew him as a hard worker. In his first years in Boston, he had learned the art of landscaping through his work experiences in the suburbs of Newton and Brookline where he had done weekend work for professional landscaping businesses. After marrying my mother, in addition to his full-time job at Harvard University, my father also had a side business where he cut lawns, planted shrubs, and tended to more than a dozen accounts. Since he now worked the night shift, Larry would grab a couple hours of sleep in the morning and from early spring through late fall head out for his second job.

My father was determined to be debt-free, to pay off their mortgage and own their home *outright*. The thought of debt frightened Larry and he very much wanted to have a sense of financial security. While his Harvard paycheck paid the bills, it didn't give him the extra money he needed to pay down their mortgage. It was never a consideration that my mother would go to work outside their home. My parents were both committed to traditional gender roles where my father earned a living, and my mother took care of the children and home. When one paycheck was not enough to achieve their financial goals, Larry created a business that supplemented his full-time income.

When my older sister Noreen and I were in the third and fourth grades, my father decided we were old enough to work summers with him. Larry owned multiple lawn mowers and he would outline the lawn and then hand-off the mowers to my sister and me so that we might walk up and down until the lawn was complete. As we cut lawns, my father edged, trimmed, and weeded. With our help, my father was able to knock off as many as three accounts in a single day. At first, our pay was a much-enjoyed donut and soda from local donut shops.

After a season, I saw my father receiving checks from his clients, which were generally for about $10 to $15. I saw the checks, which he pushed into the car ashtray, and I told my father I wanted a cut, that my sister and I should be paid. I recall my mother was upset with my father since he had immediately agreed and paid my sister and me $2 for each lawn. But Larry said he couldn't argue with my logic, that he couldn't make as much without his daughters' work. I recall placing my dollars each day in a special box and I felt quite proud to have my own money. But my feelings were quickly called into question.

After more than three years of working summers with my father my Aunt Mary and her family were visiting for a summer barbeque. I overheard her tell my father that it was shameful that he had his daughters doing physical work at our age. *You know Larry,* she said, *President Lincoln freed the slaves.* She went on to tell my father that his daughters should be enjoying their summers and Larry responded that as children they had worked much harder on the farm. *You aren't in Ireland Larry. This is America,* my aunt told him.

I recall giving that exchange serious thought. I had never felt that the work we did was inappropriate or too hard. In fact, a number of my father's clients had swimming pools and often invited my sister and me to swim when we were done, a treat we relished. One client, a Brookline widow with a substantial home that I regarded as a mansion, was especially kind.

Mrs. Sargent was an elegant woman who lived in a large, brick home with a slate roof and stunning grounds. She had a live-in maid and chauffeur, who were always very kind to my sister and me when we worked with our dad. One day I was working alone since my sister was home sick and I asked if I could use the bathroom. Mrs. Sargent welcomed me into her home, and I will never forget the sight of an indoor, water-operated elevator in the grand entry hall. Mrs. Sargent could see I was awe struck and she asked if I would like a tour of her home. I jumped at the opportunity.

As we toured, Mrs. Sargent pointed out framed photographs of her late husband with President Roosevelt and told me he was the greatest president our country had ever had. We rode the elevator together and I could hardly believe that a private residence would have such a luxury. She had her maid bring out cookies and milk and I enjoyed them in her grand dining room, which comfortably seated sixteen people. My tour concluded on the terrace where Mrs. Sargent chatted with me and told me she had a special gift she would like me to have.

At the conclusion of our special day, Mrs. Sargent brought me to her bedroom and handed me a grey velvet pouch. I opened it to find a set of pearls, and she smiled telling me that a young woman should always wear pearls on special occasions. I still have those pearls today, along with my kind memories of Mrs. Sargent. For me, going to Mrs. Sargent's home was as much a treat as going to Disney Land.

But my aunt's criticism of my father made me pause. I wondered if cutting lawns was appropriate for a grade school-aged girl. I contemplated if what is right and wrong had less to do with how we feel, and more to do with what society says about how we should feel. My aunt's criticism did not alter my father's belief that hard work was an important value to transmit to his children and contributing financially to the family was the responsibility of everyone in the family, just as it had been during his childhood in Ireland. My sister and I continued to work with my father until we got jobs of our own at fifteen and sixteen.

In the process, Larry imparted the central importance of hard work. I will never forget the day he took my sister Noreen and me to the bank to make his final mortgage payment. My father told us that *today, I own my house, and no one can ever take it from me*. He smiled and patted us on the head, telling us our hard work had helped make the day possible. My father bought us a donut after the trip to celebrate, and I recall thinking the day was better than Christmas. Larry took tremendous pride in his ability to own a home, and he valued the country that gave him the opportunity to achieve it.

America is the greatest country on earth, and don't you forget it. Larry Cummings

My father would always admit his first preference would have been to stay and farm in Ireland as his ancestors had done before him. But he was always grateful for the opportunities he and my mother had had in the United States. As children he would tell us there is no other country on earth that would take in so many people and give them the chance to work and build a future. Both Larry and Betty were grateful for the opportunities they had had and wanted to convey to their children the central importance of respect for their homeland.

My father, in particular, felt it was important to instruct his children about our country's history and each year we would take a summer vacation to an historical location. Washington D.C., Gettysburg, and the Man in the Mountain in New Hampshire were among our family trips. Larry would read every plaque and stop at every statue and tell us how important it was for us to appreciate our *great country*. In particular, Larry had an appreciation for the World War II generation and everything they sacrificed. My father would admit that he had learned little about the war while in Ireland, but since coming to America, he made a life-long commitment to learning as much as possible, reading any book and watching any program about World War II. But more than hard work and respect for our country, my parents were primarily concerned about our safety.

In this regard, Larry and Betty fully appreciated that they were not in Ireland anymore, and the dangers which presented themselves to their children had not been present when they were growing up. For example, my dad routinely cautioned us about the dangers of drugs and warned us never to leave a drink at a party, *'cause someone could slip somethin' into it*. My mother warned us about boys trying to get us alone, and I recall she particularly worried about a middle-aged man who lived with his mother in our neighborhood. *Don't go near him,* she repeatedly reminded us. But Larry also felt it was crucial to have additional protection.

Doctor, the dog has two more teeth than I do. (Larry Cummings)

Growing up we had a number of dogs, all German Shepherds, who were, first and foremost, guard dogs. My father worked nights for many years, and he worried about his wife and children being alone in the house. Having a dog that would bark, and potentially attack an intruder, was a source of comfort to my father. Typically, Larry brought home dogs from Harvard University's Medical School where animals were frequently available when they were inappropriate for research.

But my father did not adhere to local regulations to license our family pets and put tags on their collars. He thought Americans made too much fuss over pets, treating them as if they were human. But on one occasion our shepherd Prince got out of our backyard and was picked up by the local dog officer. To reclaim him, my father had to get a license for Prince, which required the dog have his requisite shots.

Waiting for the veterinarian, Larry was bewildered that animals were called into the office using the surname of the owner. When Prince Cummings was called my father begrudgingly walked our dog into the office. After his shots, the doctor informed my father that Prince had a number of health issues. Among them he said was the sad fact the dog only had two teeth. *Doctor,* my father replied, *he has two more than I do.*

After losing most of his teeth during his childhood in Ireland, Larry eventually needed false teeth after arriving in America. With health care that included a dental plan, my dad was able to finally have a full set of teeth again. But he had little sympathy for the doctor's lament about our dog Prince. Larry routinely mushed together a meal for our dogs that combined dog food and table scraps with enough water to make it easily chewed and digested. For Larry, that was royal treatment for an animal, far better than it would have enjoyed in Ireland. Prince's visit to the vet would be his first and last, and my parents always insured that our dogs remained within the boundaries of our yard after that.

Larry and Betty always struggled with the challenge of raising a family in a time and place that was foreign to them. It was natural for them to default to behaviors that were comfortable and consistent with the rural, Irish values they had learned. And there was little focus on immigrant families during the 1960s, since they did not a constitute significant percentage of the population.

When my parents were raising our family, first generation immigrants accounted for less than 5% of the U.S. population. Prior to 1965, immigration rested on a quota system that largely favored Great Britain, Ireland and Germany. New arrivals were overwhelmingly white and spoke English, easily assimilating into American society. Among my friends and neighbors, I was the only child of immigrant parents. When I was raised in the suburbs of Boston, being a child of immigrants was the exception, not a commonplace experience. The immigration landscape in America was changed, however, after the passage of the 1965 Immigration and Nationality Act.

The new law removed the quota system placing a priority on occupational skills, immigrants with families living in the U.S., and political refugees. As a consequence, immigrant numbers among Asian and Latin-American groups escalated.[120] But I was in elementary school when the law was passed, and in high school before its implications were felt. When my parents were raising their family there were no resources to guide them in uncharted territory. Aside from the relatives that had come before them, they did the best they could.

Larry and Betty were not prepared to address the challenges of raising children as we entered adolescence. They retreated, choosing not to ask questions, not to attend parent-teacher conferences, not to look at report cards, and just to hope for the best. We were expected to have jobs and pay for our clothing and expenses, which we did. We were expected to attend junior and senior high school, which we did, though they never asked about our performance. Since they couldn't identify with the world we lived in, they seemed to remove themselves from it. They also took a very Irish view on what constituted being an independent adult.

I recall my parents took a three-week trip to Ireland when I was a rising sophomore in high school. I was fifteen, and my older sister sixteen. Together, we were put in charge of my younger sister who was twelve years old. They brought my younger brother with them on their trip home, and my dad was proud to show off his son who had not been born when my family had traveled to Ireland in the 1960s. There were no cell phones at that time, nor were there phones in their family homes in Ireland. They were gone for three weeks with no contact with their teenage daughters, and never thought anything about it. They felt that my older sister and I were old enough to cook, clean and look after my youngest sister. I recall my mother left a hundred dollars in cash, hidden in

---

[120] https://www.pewresearch.org/short-reads/2020/08/20/key-findings-about-u-s-immigrants/.

the basement, so we could buy any food we might need. She also left an insurance card in case we needed medical attention.

I write this not because I argue it made them bad parents; in their minds, they were not. In their worldview entering your teen years made you an adult. My mother had finished school at fourteen and gone off to work as a servant at sixteen. My father was essentially running his family's farm at fourteen. As a consequence, Larry and Betty parented as if they were in the world they grew up in. Fortunately for them, while my sister and I did have a party, we were fairly responsible. We went to our jobs, made meals, cleaned the house, looked after my younger sister and, with the exception of a single, controlled party, stayed out of trouble.

Years later, we often shared stories with my parents about things we did that they never knew. We talked about the boys we dated behind their backs, the alcohol we drank before we reached the legal age, and the parties we attended when we said we were babysitting. While that is a familiar theme for most families, native-born and immigrant, it seemed to be more severe in ours. But in our family, it was more that our parents thought it wasn't their job to know. Once you were a teenager, you were an adult, and my parents felt if we made bad decisions, we would have to face the consequences.

My parents believed that it was their job to provide a solid foundation for their children. For them, a good parent put a roof over your head and food on the table; brought you to church; encouraged a commitment to family; insisted that you work hard; and taught you right from wrong. Once you were a teenager, you were on your own, and what you made of your life was in your own hands. They believed, as their parents did, that the early years were formative, and once a child reached adolescence, there was little more to be done. And in our early years, my father in particular, was clear about what those values should be.

For my parents, the goal was clear: recreate their Irish experience in America, to whatever extent they possibly could. They imparted the central importance of Catholicism, obedience, hard work, and appreciation of country. But try as they did, Larry and Betty could not remain in their insulated worlds.

CHAPTER EIGHTEEN:
REMOVING THE STRAITJACKET

My parents lived in an insulated world for years, choosing to stay among their *own people,* and their comfort zone of religious and cultural familiarity. But life inevitably changed as my siblings and I brought friends home that were not exclusively white, Irish Catholics, as new neighbors from disparate backgrounds moved into their neighborhood, and as my father's workplace became increasingly diverse. A pivotal time for my parents was in the 1970s.

I just don't get it, why do they want to mix everyone up? (Larry Cummings)

During the 1970s Boston was engulfed in the desegregation crisis.[121] U.S. District Judge Arthur Garrity in his 1974 ruling in *Morgan v. Hennigan* concluded that Boston's geographically segregated schools discriminated against Black students. He ordered the busing of Black students to predominantly white schools and White students to black schools in an effort to force integration. *Busing,* as it was called, was met with violent

---

121 For an overview of Boston's desegregation see, https://www.history.com/this-day-in-history/violence-in-boston-over-racial-busing.

resistance, particularly in South Boston, the city's main Irish-Catholic neighborhood. As violence escalated the National Guard was mobilized to enforce the federal desegregation order.

As a high school student, I was horrified at the images that came across the national news each evening. As an Irish Catholic, I was embarrassed by the behavior of the protesters who taunted small Black children as they rode to school. My father and I discussed the busing crisis many times and he had difficulty understanding the Judge's order. Larry believed everyone was better off staying with his or her own people. *Why,* he asked, *do they want to mix everyone up?* Larry and Betty were about to enter the post-modern, global world and their journey was a struggle.

When my father first arrived in the United States and went to work, he aligned with his Black co-workers as part of the *working class,* who had to show up, put up and shut up. He never saw skin color as a source of racism because Larry had never encountered it at home. He understood the English were racist toward the Irish, but the American experience surrounding racism was distinctly different, and Larry and his family soon learned about the Black experience in the country they now called home.

It wasn't long before the Cummings family understood that racism in America was a tragic and violent legacy of slavery. While Larry and his siblings fully appreciated the fallout of British colonialism, they came to appreciate that in the States, colonialism had sowed the seeds of a brand of racism that was raw and ubiquitous in contemporary America. Where Ignatiev had argued it was a conscious choice in *How the Irish Became White*,[122] I have posited that it was less a choice than a gradual

---

122 Ignatiev. See Chapter 11.

absorption. As my parents and their extended family moved from the city to the primarily white suburbs, they absorbed America's racist assumptions. By the time the busing crisis was at its peak in Boston during the 1970s, Larry no longer identified with his former, Black co-workers. He and his siblings were fully white Americans who internalized all the supremacist assumptions that accompanied their newfound status.

But the images that poured across our television set each evening during the 1970s could not be denied, dismissed or explained away. While Boston was not the only city in America with profound issues of racism, it was the most visible. And for my parents, it forced a reckoning between what they knew, what they had abandoned, and where they would go as Irish Americans.

My parents, especially my father, came to appreciate that part of their journey to the suburbs, home ownership and middle-class America had led them to embrace racist assumptions that they did not have when they emigrated. The 1970s was a time when my parents came face-to-face with those assumptions and as the glaring images of busing poured into our living room, they were uncomfortably aware that we were eleven miles away from a national disgrace. When I asked my parents for permission to skip school to join a protest in support of school integration and racial equality, they gave me their support. Unlearning acquired assumptions took time, and my parents' journey was also evident in other aspects of cultural changes.

Sure, Kathy, she is pretty enough to get a man. (Betty Cummings)

During graduate school I was in a study group with a number of fellow students, including a woman who was a lesbian. My mother had the occasion to meet her at my home when my friend stopped by to return a book she had borrowed. After my friend left my mother asked me if she were married or had a boyfriend. I told her that she had a girlfriend, that she was a lesbian. Betty was shocked, *sure Kathy,* she said, *she is pretty enough to get a man.*

My parents had great difficulty coming to terms with homosexuality. My father would say *it just isn't natural.* But as time went on, they both came to develop a greater understanding for sexual complexity. The turning point came when my father attended the funeral of a long-term co-worker.

Larry was promoted to a supervisory role in his mid-fifties at Harvard University and shared an office with another male supervisor. Together, they managed two teams for more than a decade. The two men ate lunch together five days a week and often went out on Friday evenings after work for a pint. Like my father, his fellow supervisor was a white, middle-aged, Irish Catholic. Larry told us he was a *confirmed bachelor,* and never wanted to marry. Sadly, his friend and colleague died suddenly as a consequence of heart issues.

My parents attended the wake and funeral of my dad's good friend and fellow supervisor where they were introduced to the deceased's roommate, someone my father had never heard his friend even mention in conversation. As it turned out, the two men had been partners for many years, sharing a home and their lives together. It was in that moment that my father learned that his good friend and coworker had been homosexual. Larry told me he couldn't believe it. *Why,* he asked, *wouldn't he tell me?* I told my father he likely did not because he couldn't trust his potential reaction. *Imagine,* I said to my dad, *if you had to hide your relationship with mom, never put a picture on your desk, keep your life together a secret from even those closest around you?*

My father looked tragically sad and was quiet for a long time. This was a man he could relate to in every way except his sexuality, and for the first time it sunk in. Many weeks later, watching a news report about a gay man who was attacked for his sexuality, my father said *Jesus, people are all just people. We all want the same things out of life. Why can't people be kinder and more acceptin'?*

My parents' eventual acceptance of sexual diversity and other causes, like reproductive rights, forced a reconciliation with their faith. While both of my parents tenaciously clung to their belief in God and an afterlife, they eventually abandoned the Bible as the literal word of God. They continued to attend mass, receive communion, and steadfastly await their eternal salvation where they would be reunited with their families in Heaven. At the same time, my father voted Democrat and he and my mother supported liberal causes. In the process Larry and Betty's faith no longer dictated their lives, rather their religious beliefs spiritually enhanced it. The straitjacket formed by strict Irish Catholicism and rural parochialism was loosening. The defining moment for my parents, however, came when Larry was about to retire.

They are the hardest workers I know. (Larry Cummings)

After more than forty years as an employee of Harvard University, my father lost his job when he and his staff were let go due to outsourcing. Larry had been promoted to boss and ran a small department that took care of heating and cooling systems. Harvard did a cost assessment and concluded that it was cheaper to outsource the work rather than pay salaries and benefits to employees. It was a trend witnessed across the country, and it mentally devastated my father.

Like many Americans in those times, Larry believed that loyalty and hard work would be rewarded with job security until he retired. In his early sixties at the time, my father called me crying with disbelief. Not since our departure from Ireland in the 1960s had I witnessed my father cry. Over the phone, he wailed with such a vengeance that I initially thought he must be calling to tell me that my mother was dead. I went to console my father and later helped him put a resume together. In just a few months he got a job as a supervisor of a maintenance crew at Jude Baker Children's Center in Boston.

There, Larry supervised a crew of six, five men and one woman, all of whom were originally from Puerto Rico. Before he started the job, Larry was concerned that he might not have much in common with his new staff. But as he got to know them, however, my father was impressed. Larry found his crew to be hard-working, talented, and gracious people. He would later proudly say, *they are the hardest workers I know,* lofty praise from a man who had a high bar in what constituted hard work. His team became his friends, and one of his staff invited him to his wedding. Since I had minored in Spanish in college my father asked me to interpret the invitation, which was written in the groom's native language. He and my mother went to the wedding, and they told me it was the most fun they had ever had at a reception. My father was especially proud to tell me that the groom's mother asked him to dance and told him he was the best boss her son had ever had.

When my father was ready to retire, he was asked by administration if a member of his staff might be able to succeed him. Larry didn't hesitate, and firmly endorsed the sole female who also happened to be homosexual. *They are all good, but she is the best of the lot,* he told me. After several weeks of training, Larry retired, and his former female employee replaced him as boss.

A few weeks later I joined my parents at their home for dinner along with their guests of honor, the woman of color who replaced my father as supervisor and her lesbian partner. I watched my parents make a fuss over their guests just as they had done all those years ago when Father Cullinane came to dinner. I smiled and privately reflected that my parents had come a long way, both spiritually and emotionally. The straitjackets they had worn when they arrived in America were gone.

As senior citizens, Betty and Larry settled into an in-law suite in my brother and sister-in-law's home in Kingston, 45 miles south of Boston. Known to their ten grandchildren as Nana and Pop, they continued to share their stories and encouraged values that they regarded as central to realizing a meaningful life. First among them was hard work.

Larry was intent on explaining to his grandchildren why his *make sure your toilets are the cleanest* philosophy was key to lifelong success. My father would tell them no one owes you anything in life, you have to go out and earn it. What you did was not important to Larry, it was your commitment to what you did that mattered. Pop would tell each grandchild that he was not a good student, that he had been called a *dummy* in school, but he made it and did far better than anyone could have imagined, because he worked harder than the *next guy*.

Today, his grandchildren work at a variety of careers from restaurant ownership to education to commercial painting. Each child possesses a strong work ethic, and whenever my siblings and I comment on our children's work they will say, *just like Pop*. And while my mother certainly encouraged hard work, she also stressed the central importance of family.

Betty's tenuous relationship with her family line made her intensely committed to insuring strong family bonds. Gathering for holidays and life events was my mother's first priority. Our children can look back on years of family events where their grandparents presided at the head of the table. To this day, her legacy continues, though we often joke that the menu is much improved since we have moved beyond over-cooked beef and soggy vegetables.

As our families expanded, my parents welcomed newcomers and embraced the diversity of their new world. They warmly accepted their grandchildren's partners and accepted that premarital sex and sexual differences were not *sins,* but a part of the human experience. They did tend to think, however, that my siblings and I *spoiled our kids* too much. Both Larry and Betty rejected the idea that kids be given participation trophies, and felt they needed more responsibility and fewer material comforts.

At the same time, Larry and Betty recognized that there were some practices, like corporal punishment, that should be abandoned. My children know my favorite quote is from Maya Angelou when she said, *you did what you knew, and when you knew better, you did better.*[123] I firmly believe this sentiment applies to values as they are transmitted from one generation to the next. We learn, reevaluate and in the process, keep what works, and abandon what does not.

For my parents, they kept their faith in God, but abandoned Catholic dogma that worked against their new values. As opposed to their childhoods when their faith was a source of fear and potential punishment, in their senior years it was a source of

---

[123] https://www.goodhousekeeping.com/life/g39178842/maya-angelou-quotes/?slide=35

inspiration and comfort. Religious imagery on their walls gave way to framed photographs from family gatherings, which brought a smile to their faces, and enhanced their day-to-day lives.

And for my mother, Betty found validation in sharing her birth story with her children and grandchildren. My mother lifted a shroud of secrecy and the heavy emotional burden she had carried for so many years. In its place, she found acceptance and love in the womb of the family she held dear.

My parents were born into the homogeneity of Ireland but died in a world where diversity was embraced and celebrated. In the process, they shed their emotional and intellectual straitjackets, and found contentment in their senior years, surrounded by their children and grandchildren. Larry and Betty kept what worked for them and discarded what worked against them.

Today, their grandchildren experience a rich complexity of opportunity and encounter very different challenges than what Larry and Betty had experienced. All of them were born in the post-modern world where the economy was global, unskilled labor that paid a living wage was contracting, and information exchange was instantaneous. Today, my grandchildren have every moment of their lives captured and available on social media; and perhaps, in recounting their lives, books like this will no longer be necessary.

But I am confident that my parents would be thrilled that the great grandchildren they never met will read about our family's history. More than any of their children, I embraced values that were anathema to them during their upbringings in Ireland. But my parents came to embrace and celebrate new, modern values and they were both eager to participate in research for this book, for which I am grateful. While I am not sure Larry and Betty fully appreciated that we all have much to learn from connecting with the stories of ordinary lives, I would argue that the rich fabric of our historical narrative cannot be adequately woven without the recognition that every voice has value.

EPILOGUE

"The Kerry girl," my mother Elizabeth, and my father, Lawrence Kilcommins, made their home in Boston and later in the town of Braintree, eleven miles south of the city. There, they raised their family with the Cummings name, and built a foundation for the future. My dad died at the age of 82 leaving my mother in their in-law apartment, connected to family in the Irish tradition. Sadly, my mother developed Alzheimer's Disease at the age of 85 and spent the last days of her life in a memory-care facility near my brother and sister-in-law's home.

Over the course of their marriage my parents returned *home* as often as finances and life circumstances allowed. Together, they raised four children, three daughters and a son, and joyfully welcomed their ten grandchildren into the world. My father was an American citizen who often waxed nostalgically about what life would have been like had he raised his family in the old country. My mother never became an American citizen, although she never entertained the idea of returning *home* for good.

My uncle Paddy Kilcommins lives alone today on the family farm in Bornacurra. His oldest son, Michael, owns an adjoining farm, and he, his wife Olive and children see my uncle regularly.

My uncle's wife, Mary, died from breast cancer about a decade after my grandmother, Nora, passed. Unlike Paddy's siblings, his children, Michael, Maura, Theresa, and Claire remained in Ireland. The inclusion of Ireland in the European Union and the tremendous changes, politically and economically, ushered in good times for my cousins. All four are married with children and doing well, and today they are each making their lives in Ireland, never having contemplated a move across *the pond*.

My father and mother regularly attended mass and my father always clung to his medal of St. Anthony. Of their four children, only their son is a practicing Catholic. The faith that shaped their lives did not similarly shape the lives of their three daughters.

The lad, who shared a bed with three brothers and left begrudgingly for England making his permanent home in America, lived a simple life grounded in hard-work, faith in God and family. Betty made peace with her *shameful secret* by removing it from the dark, sharing it, and owning her bravery in doing so. Both my parents arrived in America with their cultural straitjackets and had successfully shed them by their senior years. Born Lawrence Kilcommins, my father lived as Larry Cummings with Elizabeth his Kerry girl in the golden years of what had been a long, challenging and eventful journey from the top of the Irish bog to Boston.

Larry and Betty, engagement photo, 1956

Larry's childhood home, with his grandparents, aunt and two uncles, 1921

Nora and Paddy on their 40th wedding anniversary, 1963

Larry and his siblings, Paddy, Tom, John, Peggy, Mike and Mary, 1960s

Peggy, Betty, Larry, Kay (John's wife), Tom, Sheila (Tom's wife), Noreen (Mike's wife), Mike, Mary and John, 2000

Larry and Paddy, 2009

Larry and Betty with their children and partners, 2015

Larry and Betty's grandchildren, 2021

Nora and Paddy's headstone in Bornacurra

The Kilcommins family home today

Made in the USA
Columbia, SC
14 November 2024

46381719R00128